OVERSIGHT OF THE CYBERSECURITY ACT OF 2015

HEARING

BEFORE THE

SUBCOMMITTEE ON CYBERSECURITY, INFRASTRUCTURE PROTECTION, AND SECURITY TECHNOLOGIES

OF THE

COMMITTEE ON HOMELAND SECURITY HOUSE OF REPRESENTATIVES

ONE HUNDRED FOURTEENTH CONGRESS

SECOND SESSION

JUNE 15, 2016

Serial No. 114–76

Printed for the use of the Committee on Homeland Security

Available via the World Wide Web: http://www.gpo.gov/fdsys/

U.S. GOVERNMENT PUBLISHING OFFICE

24–379 PDF   WASHINGTON : 2017

For sale by the Superintendent of Documents, U.S. Government Publishing Office
Internet: bookstore.gpo.gov Phone: toll free (866) 512–1800; DC area (202) 512–1800
Fax: (202) 512–2104 Mail: Stop IDCC, Washington, DC 20402–0001

COMMITTEE ON HOMELAND SECURITY

MICHAEL T. MCCAUL, Texas, *Chairman*

LAMAR SMITH, Texas
PETER T. KING, New York
MIKE ROGERS, Alabama
CANDICE S. MILLER, Michigan, *Vice Chair*
JEFF DUNCAN, South Carolina
TOM MARINO, Pennsylvania
LOU BARLETTA, Pennsylvania
SCOTT PERRY, Pennsylvania
CURT CLAWSON, Florida
JOHN KATKO, New York
WILL HURD, Texas
EARL L. "BUDDY" CARTER, Georgia
MARK WALKER, North Carolina
BARRY LOUDERMILK, Georgia
MARTHA MCSALLY, Arizona
JOHN RATCLIFFE, Texas
DANIEL M. DONOVAN, JR., New York

BENNIE G. THOMPSON, Mississippi
LORETTA SANCHEZ, California
SHEILA JACKSON LEE, Texas
JAMES R. LANGEVIN, Rhode Island
BRIAN HIGGINS, New York
CEDRIC L. RICHMOND, Louisiana
WILLIAM R. KEATING, Massachusetts
DONALD M. PAYNE, JR., New Jersey
FILEMON VELA, Texas
BONNIE WATSON COLEMAN, New Jersey
KATHLEEN M. RICE, New York
NORMA J. TORRES, California

BRENDAN P. SHIELDS, *Staff Director*
JOAN V. O'HARA, *General Counsel*
MICHAEL S. TWINCHEK, *Chief Clerk*
I. LANIER AVANT, *Minority Staff Director*

———

SUBCOMMITTEE ON CYBERSECURITY, INFRASTRUCTURE PROTECTION, AND SECURITY TECHNOLOGIES

JOHN RATCLIFFE, Texas, *Chairman*

PETER T. KING, New York
TOM MARINO, Pennsylvania
SCOTT PERRY, Pennsylvania
CURT CLAWSON, Florida
DANIEL M. DONOVAN, JR., New York
MICHAEL T. MCCAUL, Texas *(ex officio)*

CEDRIC L. RICHMOND, Louisiana
LORETTA SANCHEZ, California
SHEILA JACKSON LEE, Texas
JAMES R. LANGEVIN, Rhode Island
BENNIE G. THOMPSON, Mississippi *(ex officio)*

BRETT DEWITT, *Subcommittee Staff Director*
KATIE RASHID, *Subcommittee Clerk*
CHRISTOPHER SCHEPIS, *Minority Subcommittee Staff Director*

(II)

CONTENTS

IV

OVERSIGHT OF THE CYBERSECURITY ACT OF 2015

Wednesday, June 15, 2016

U.S. House of Representatives,
Committee on Homeland Security,
Subcommittee on Cybersecurity, Infrastructure
Protection, and Security Technologies,
Washington, DC.

The subcommittee met, pursuant to notice, at 10:12 a.m., in Room 311, Cannon House Office Building, Hon. John Ratcliffe (Chairman of the subcommittee) presiding.

Present: Representatives Ratcliffe, McCaul, Perry, Clawson, Donovan, Richmond, Thompson, Sanchez, Jackson Lee, and Langevin.

Mr. RATCLIFFE. Pursuant to committee rule 5(a), I now convene the Subcommittee on Cybersecurity, Infrastructure Protection, and Security Technologies with the concurrence of the Ranking Member.

Before we begin this morning, I would be remiss if I didn't again mention the Orlando terrorist attack that killed 49 innocent victims, the largest attack in the United States since 9/11. I would ask that we would open with a moment of silence in remembrance of the victims and their families. Thank you.

The subcommittee meets today to fulfill its obligation and oversight responsibility of examining the implementation of the Cybersecurity Act of 2015 since its passage last year, and to look at the necessary steps going forward to strengthen our Nation's cyber defenses.

Congress' job doesn't end when a piece of legislation is signed into law, and that is especially true when it comes to cybersecurity legislation. Continued oversight is essential to making sure that the bill is implemented in a manner that actually improves our cyber defenses. If agency guidance isn't clear, if tweaks need to be made, we want to hear that feedback and we want to address those concerns.

For that reason, we are pleased to be joined today by a distinguished panel of industry experts to discuss this very important issue.

Pushing the Cybersecurity Act of 2015 across the finish line last year was a significant accomplishment that was years in the making. During that time, these witnesses that are here today and others representing critical sectors devoted substantial energy to collaborate with policy makers like me on the best path forward. Hundreds of hours of stakeholder outreach were conducted across literally every relevant industry group: Energy, health care, financial services, technology, telecom, retail, you name it. In the end, this bill recognized many of the practices that were already being deployed by these industry groups and codified them into law, while providing important rules for the road, as well.

My objective is to maintain that same posture as we assess the implementation of the Cybersecurity Act of 2015. This law recognizes the role of DHS's National Cybersecurity and Communications Integration Center, the NCCIC, as the civilian portal for the sharing of cyber threat indicators. The key aim was to see that our cyber threat indicators containing critical information about the nature, methodology, source, and scope of cyber attacks would be shared with other parties, so they, in turn, could fortify their own networks against future intrusions.

In response to the devastating attack on the Office of Personnel Management, this law also bolsters DHS's ability to deploy intrusion detection and prevention capabilities across the Federal Government. I think we can all agree that the need for stronger cybersecurity posture is clear. Every day, our country is facing digital intrusions from criminals and hacktivists, terrorists, nation-states. Cybersecurity is National security. The impacts of those intrusions are being felt everywhere, from kitchen tables to boardroom tables across American companies.

We can't tolerate acts of cyber threat and cyber warfare, especially when they result in the theft of intellectual property and innovation, and put our Nation's critical infrastructure at risk. We can't sit idly by while escalating ransomware attacks on our hospitals and our health care providers threaten our citizens by locking out access to their medical records.

Cybersecurity breaches and data manipulation can undermine consumer confidence and they can damage a company's hard-earned reputation in just a matter of seconds. While we have yet to see a major corporation completely collapse due to a cyber attack, the possibility is no longer science fiction. One can only imagine the turmoil that would be caused if Americans suddenly found out that their checking accounts had all been drained. The loss of trust in our financial system would cause an economic meltdown.

Nearly a third of CEOs surveyed recently identified cybersecurity as the largest issue impacting their companies today, and only half of those say they are fully prepared for a cyber event.

We have learned that there are only two types of companies: Those who have been hacked and those who don't know yet that they have been hacked. Information sharing between companies, the Government, and critical sectors improves our ability to defend against all of these attacks.

Beyond the impact on the private sector, safeguarding cyber space is also one of the great National security challenges of our time. The American people recognize this. In fact, in a recent Pew Research poll, Americans named cybersecurity as their second-biggest perceived threat only to ISIS. Imagine a catastrophic cyber attack on our gas pipelines or the power grid. Such an assault on our critical infrastructure could cripple our economy and weaken our ability to defend the United States.

Our adversaries are right now hard at work developing and refining cyber attack capabilities and they are using them to intimidate our Government and to threaten our people. But the threat extends beyond the industrial engines that drive our economy, right into the homes of the American people themselves. Criminals and countries alike can now use cyber attacks to raid American savings accounts or steal their personal health records. The recent breach at Anthem last year demonstrated the very real capability and intent of bad actors to prey upon Americans' most sensitive information.

We can't leave the American people, the American economy, and our critical infrastructure to fend for itself. This is why Congress passed the Cybersecurity Act of 2015. Information is the currency of today's age, and we have to constantly work together across all sectors if we expect to stay one step ahead of our adversaries on this new battlefield.

Congress must utilize rigorous oversight to ensure that DHS is fulfilling its mission to better protect our networks, and that's why we are all here today.

I want to thank all the witnesses for testifying before our subcommittee, and I look forward to your testimony.

[The statement of Chairman Ratcliffe follows:]

STATEMENT OF CHAIRMAN JOHN RATCLIFFE

The subcommittee meets today to fulfill its oversight responsibility of examining implementation of the Cybersecurity Act of 2015 since its passage last year, and to look at necessary steps going forward to strengthen our Nation's cyber defenses.

Congress' job doesn't end when a piece of legislation is signed into law, and that is especially true when it comes to cybersecurity legislation. Continued oversight is essential to making sure the bill is implemented in a manner that actually improves our cyber defenses. If agency guidance isn't clear, if tweaks need to be made, we want to hear that feedback and address those concerns.

For that reason, we are pleased to be joined by a distinguished panel of industry experts to discuss this very important issue.

Pushing the Cybersecurity Act of 2015 across the finish line last year was a significant accomplishment that was years in the making. During that time, these witnesses and others representing critical sectors devoted substantial energy to collaborate with policy makers on the best path forward.

Hundreds of hours of stakeholder outreach were conducted across every relevant industry group—energy, health care, financial services, technology, telecom, defense, retail, you name it.

In the end, the bill recognized many of the practices already deployed by these groups and codified them into law, while providing important rules of the road.

My objective is to maintain that posture as we assess the implementation of the Cybersecurity Act of 2015.

The bill recognized the role of DHS's National Cybersecurity & Communications Integration Center, or NCCIC, as the civilian portal for the sharing of cyber threat indicators. The key aim was to see cyber threat indicators—which contain critical information about the nature, methodology, source, and scope of cyber attacks—shared with other parties so they can, in turn, fortify their own networks against future intrusion.

In response to the devastating attack on OPM, the law also bolstered DHS's ability to deploy intrusion detection and prevention capabilities across the Federal Government.

The need for a stronger cybersecurity posture is clear. Every day our country faces digital intrusions from criminals, hacktivists, terrorists, and nation-States like Russia, China, and Iran. Cybersecurity is National security, and the impacts of those intrusions are felt everywhere—from kitchen tables to American businesses.

We cannot tolerate acts of cyber theft and cyber warfare, especially when they result in the theft of intellectual property and innovation, and put our Nation's critical infrastructure at risk.

We cannot sit idly by while escalating ransomware attacks on hospitals and health care providers threaten our citizens by locking out access to medical records.

Cybersecurity breaches and data manipulation can undermine consumer confidence and damage a company's hard-earned reputation in a matter of seconds. And while we have yet to see a major corporation completely collapse due to a cyber attack, the possibility is no longer science fiction. One can only imagine the turmoil that would be caused should suddenly Americans' checking accounts be drained. Loss of trust in our financial system would cause an economic meltdown.

Nearly a third of CEOs surveyed identify cybersecurity as the largest issue impacting their companies today, and only half say they are fully prepared for a cyber event. There are two types of companies: Those who have been hacked and those who don't know they have been hacked. This is why Congress passed the Cybersecurity Act last year. Information sharing between companies, the Government, and critical sectors improves our ability to defend against these attacks.

Beyond the impact on the private sector, safeguarding cyber space is also one of the great National security challenges of our time—and the American people recognize this. In fact, in a recent Pew Research Poll, Americans named cybersecurity as their second biggest perceived threat only to ISIS.

Imagine a catastrophic cyber attack on our gas pipelines or the power grid. Such assaults on our critical infrastructure could cripple our economy and weaken our ability to defend the United States. Our adversaries are hard at work developing and refining cyber attack capabilities, and they are using them to intimidate our Government and threaten our people.

But the threat extends beyond the industrial engines that drive our economy, to the homes of Americans themselves. Criminals and countries alike can use cyber attacks to raid Americans' savings accounts or steal their personal health records. The recent breach of Anthem demonstrated the very real capability and intent of bad actors to prey upon Americans' most sensitive information.

We cannot leave the American people, the American economy, and our critical infrastructure to fend for itself.

That's why Congress passed the Cybersecurity Act of 2015. This new law strengthens DHS's ability to more effectively secure Government networks and incentivizes the sharing of cyber threat indicators among critical sectors and with the Government to bolster protections from future attacks.

Information is the currency of today's age, and we must constantly work together across all sectors if we expect to stay one step ahead of the adversaries on this new battlefield.

Congress must utilize rigorous oversight to ensure that DHS is fulfilling its mission to better protect our networks, and that's why we're here today.

I want to thank the witnesses for testifying before this subcommittee and I look forward to your testimony.

Mr. RATCLIFFE. The Chair now recognizes the Chairman of the full committee, the gentleman from Texas, Mr. McCaul, for his opening statement.

Chairman MCCAUL. I thank the Chairman for holding this important hearing today.

Before I start, I would like to say a few words about the tragic events Sunday in Orlando. Our thoughts and prayers go out to the victims and their families. Our deepest gratitude goes out to the first responders who helped save so many lives.

It was the deadliest attack on the United States homeland since 9/11. But our response has shown that Americans are resilient and will not be intimidated by extremists.

Yesterday, I moderated a Classified briefing on the investigation with the Secretary of Homeland Security, the director of the FBI, and the National Counter Terrorism Center. In the coming months, we will continue to seek answers and have an oversight hearing on this very important issue. We will also take action to protect our country and prevent such an attack from ever happening again.

The events in Orlando are a reminder that our Nation is being targeted by those who want to undermine our freedom and diminish our prosperity.

But the threat is not just from kinetic terrorists. Today we will discuss how our Nation is also being targeted and attacked in real time by faceless intruders across the web. As we speak, a war is being waged against us in cyber space. Criminals, hacktivists, violent extremists and nation-states are infiltrating our networks and infecting our systems.

Their motives are to deceive, steal, and destroy, and the impacts of their attacks are felt everywhere, from our kitchen tables to our corporate boardrooms. This committee has made our Nation's cybersecurity a top priority. In recent years we passed a number of landmark cybersecurity bills.

First, we established a Federal civilian interface at the National Cybersecurity and Communications Immigration Center, or NCCIC, to facilitate cyber threat information sharing. This allows the Government to communicate more effectively across the 16 critical infrastructure sectors and with the private sector, with liability protection.

Second, we laid down the rules of the road regarding how information is shared, making sure these data exchanges are efficient, timely, and secure.

Third, we put in place measures to keep Americans' rights and personal information protected.

Fourth, we made sure that DHS was able to hire and retain top cybersecurity talent, because we cannot protect our networks without a cyber work force that is smart and aggressive.

And fifth, we enhanced the Department's ability to prevent, respond to, and recover from cyber incidents on Federal networks.

Those measures went a long way in helping us secure our systems. But even with the fundamentals in place, we still have major vulnerabilities, especially lack of information sharing. After 9/11, we learned that if our agencies did not connect the dots, we could not stop attacks.

The same principle applies to cyber threats. If no one shares data, everyone is less secure and intrusions go undetected.

We realized that companies were very hesitant to share this sensitive data, so last year we drafted and passed the Cybersecurity Act to get the information flowing. The law now provides liability protection so that companies and other organizations can more freely exchange threat indicators.

This includes Government-to-private information sharing, but also, importantly, private-to-private sharing. The legislation was a major win for security and privacy, allowing companies to secure their networks and keep hackers away from our bank accounts, health records, and other sensitive information.

But we cannot be satisfied with this progress. We have got to be aggressive, as our adversaries are. We should aim to stay a step ahead of them at every turn.

So I hope our witnesses, and I want to thank our witnesses for being here today, but I hope you will help us understand how we can do exactly that, how can we effectively implement this law to enhance America's digital defenses. I am very interested as well to see how this program is working at the Department and what this committee can do to enhance and strengthen their efforts.

So with that, Mr. Chairman, I yield back.

[The statement of Chairman McCaul follows:]

STATEMENT OF CHAIRMAN MICHAEL T. MCCAUL

Before I start today, I would like to say a few words about the tragic events in Orlando. Our thoughts and prayers go out to the victims and their families, and our deepest gratitude goes out to the first responders who helped save lives.

It was the deadliest terrorist attack on the U.S. homeland since 9/11, but our response has shown that Americans are resilient and will not be intimidated by extremists.

Yesterday I moderated a Classified briefing on the investigation with the heads of DHS, the FBI, and the National Counterterrorism Center, and in the coming months we will continue to seek answers. We will also take action to protect our country and prevent such an attack from happening again.

The events in Orlando are a reminder that our Nation is being targeted by those who want to undermine our freedom and diminish our prosperity.

But the threat is not just from terrorists. Today we will discuss how our Nation is also being targeted and attacked—in real time—by faceless intruders across the web.

As we speak, a war is being waged against us in cyber space. Criminals, hacktivists, violent extremists, and nation-states are infiltrating our networks and infecting our systems. Their motives are to deceive, steal, and destroy, and the impacts of their attacks are felt everywhere—from our kitchen tables to corporate board rooms.

This committee has made our Nation's cybersecurity a top priority, and in recent years we have passed a number of landmark cybersecurity bills.

First, we established a Federal civilian interface at the National Cybersecurity and Communications Integration Center, or NCCIC, to facilitate cyber-threat information sharing.

This allows the Government to communicate more effectively across 16 critical infrastructure sectors and with the private sector.

Second, we laid down the rules of the road regarding how information is shared—making sure data exchanges are efficient, timely, and secure.

Third, we put in place measures to keep Americans' rights and personal information protected.

Fourth, we made sure DHS was able to hire and retain top cybersecurity talent, because we cannot protect our networks without a cyber workforce that is smart and aggressive.

And fifth, we enhanced the Department's ability to prevent, respond to, and recover from cyber incidents on Federal networks.

Those measures went a long way in helping us secure our systems. But even with the fundamentals in place, we still saw major vulnerabilities, especially the lack of information sharing.

After 9/11, we learned that if our agencies did not connect the dots, we could not stop attacks.

The same principle applies to cyber threats. If no one shares data, everyone is less secure and intrusions go undetected.

We realized that companies were very hesitant to share their sensitive data, so last year we drafted and passed the Cybersecurity Act of 2015 to get the information flowing.

The law now provides liability protections so that companies and other organizations can more freely exchange threat indicators. This includes "Government-to-private" information sharing and "private-to-private" sharing.

The legislation was a major win for security and privacy, allowing companies to secure their networks and keep hackers away from our bank accounts, health records, and other sensitive information.

But we cannot be satisfied with this progress. We've got to be as aggressive as our adversaries—and we should aim to stay a step ahead of them.

I hope today our witnesses will help us understand how we can do exactly that—and how we can effectively implement this law to enhance America's digital defenses.

Thank you.

Mr. RATCLIFFE. Thank you, Mr. Chairman, and thank you for your leadership on this issue.

Other Members of the committee are reminded that opening statements may be submitted for the record.

[The statements of Ranking Member Thompson and Hon. Jackson Lee follow:]

STATEMENT OF RANKING MEMBER BENNIE G. THOMPSON

JUNE 15, 2016

Today, the subcommittee turns its attention to another pressing issue: Securing our cyber networks. Cyber threats are constantly evolving. While a few years ago, critical infrastructure operators were primarily concerned about spear-phishing and DDOS attacks, today, the threat of ransomware attacks are front-of-mind. Over the past year, the proliferation of ransomware attacks, where networks of a hospital system, Government agency, or utility are held hostage for electronic payments, has reached epidemic proportions.

In March, DHS reported that over the past year, there have been 321 incidents of "ransomware-related activity" affecting 29 Federal networks. The FBI Internet Crime Complaint Center, for its part, has acknowledged that over the last decade, of the $58 million in financial damage attributable to such attacks, attacks in just the last year account for $24 million in damage.

With more Americans coming to embrace the Internet of Things, the disruptive and damaging effects of ransomware and other innovative modes of attack deployed by hackers have the potential to inflict significant damage to our Nation.

To counter this threat, we must redouble our efforts to promote cyber hygiene practices, encryption, and information sharing. The enactment of the "Cybersecurity Act" in December provides for the sharing of information on cybersecurity threats and defensive measures between the Government and the private sector and within the private sector.

Privacy, liability, and anti-trust provisions that are universally understood as essential to the timely sharing of cyber threat information are part of this law. Under the Act, the epicenter for such activity is, of course, the National Cybersecurity and Communications Integration Center.

I am interested in exploring two key mandates in the Act. First, I want to hear from industry stakeholders how they see the launch of the "Automated Indicator Sharing" capability, as required under the Act, impacting information sharing.

Second, I would like to hear the witnesses' perspective on how well DHS is carrying out the requirement to periodically share, through publication and targeted outreach, cybersecurity best practices in a manner that gives "attention to accessibility and implementation challenges faced by small businesses."

Before I close, I would like to note that, this past week, I was heartened to see how the United States stacks up to other nations when it comes to vulnerability to hacking.

The United States was ranked fourteenth on the "National Exposure Index," a worldwide comparative analysis of vulnerability to cyber attacks and cyber crime that is based on the scanning of millions of internet channels for vulnerabilities such as unencrypted and plain text services.

While it is good to see that the United States is less vulnerable than Brussels, Australia, France, and China—countries on the list found to have weak authentication and encryption practices—now is not the time to rest on our laurels.

STATEMENT OF HONORABLE SHEILA JACKSON LEE

Chairman Ratcliffe and Ranking Member Richmond, thank you for holding this morning's hearing entitled "Oversight of the Cybersecurity Act of 2015."

This hearing is an opportunity to receive testimony regarding implementation of the Cybersecurity Act of 2015, enacted on December 18, 2015, which was intended to resolve long-standing issues that prevented private-sector participants from sharing information on cyber threats with the Federal Government or with each other.

I look forward to hearing from today's witnesses: Mr. Matthew J. Eggers—senior director, National Security and Emergency Preparedness, U.S. Chamber of Commerce; Mr. Robert H. Mayer—vice president, Industry and State Affairs, U.S. Telecom Association; Mr. Mark Clancy—chief executive officer, Soltra; Mr. Mordecai Rosen—general manager, Security Business Unit, CA Technologies; and Ms. Ola Sage—founder and chief executive officer, eManagement.

As Ranking Member of the Judiciary Subcommittee on Crime, Terrorism, Homeland Security and Investigations and a senior member of the Committee on Homeland Security, I am a strong believer in the legislative process as the best path for addressing the most complex issues of the digital communication age.

The Cybersecurity Act of 2015 did not follow regular order to become law—it was included in the Omnibus Appropriations bill passed at the end of last year.

The bill encourages private companies to voluntarily share information about cyber threats with each other as well as the Government and includes the authorization of information sharing and its impacts on privacy and civil liberties; risks of misuse by the Federal Government or the private sector; and effects of proposed liability protections for companies and entities who participate in cybersecurity information sharing.

The law requires the U.S. Attorney General and Secretary of Homeland Security to publish guidelines, and jointly submit to Congress interim CISA policies and procedures by February 16, 2016, and publish final policies and procedures by June 15, 2016, to assist businesses in identifying information that would qualify as a cyber threat indicator and eliminating personal information from shared cyber threat information.

These guidelines will seek to: (1) Identify cyber threat indicators that contain personal information and are unlikely to directly relate to a cybersecurity threat, and, (2) identify types of information that is protected under privacy laws and are unlikely to directly relate to a cybersecurity threat.

THE CYBERSECURITY AND INFORMATION-SHARING LEGISLATION

The law broadly authorizes the Federal Government to share Unclassified "cyber threat indicators" and "defensive measures" technical data that indicates how networks have been attacked, and how such attacks have been successfully detected, prevented, or mitigated.

The law authorizes the sharing of Unclassified information among Federal agencies, as well as with businesses and the public.

Classified cyber threat information, in contrast, may be shared outside the Government only with entities that have appropriate security clearances.

Vulnerabilities in computing products are the chief method used by data thieves and terrorists to breach computing systems.

Since 2005 to the present, the Privacy Rights Clearinghouse, reports that 895,886,345 records have been breached.

Entities and their customers that have fallen victim to data breaches range in size from small businesses to major corporations and Federal Government agencies, including:

- The IRS—101,000 the agency block payments to data thieves who used stolen identity information from elsewhere to generate pins using stolen Social Security Numbers (date reported 2/10/2016).
- Scottrade—lost over 4 million records (October 1, 2015).
- Excellus Blue Cross Blue Shield—lost over 10 million patient records (September 10, 2015).
- Office of Personnel Management (OPM)—lost over 21.5 million Government employee or former employee records (June 4, 2015).

Most data breach reports include no details on the number of records breached or stolen.

There is no law that requires companies to report breaches, but there are laws that require reports to consumers when their personal information may have been lost or stolen.

Identifying and closing vulnerabilities in software and firmware IS one important means of securing systems from threats.

The link between commercially available computing devices and our Nation's critical infrastructure lies in the role of products in ensuring the proper maintenance and operation of critical infrastructure.

RANSOMWARE AND HACKING ACTIVITY

The latest threat from cyber hackers is ransomware.

Bad actors find vulnerabilities in a computer or computing network and use it to introduce an encryption application that locks the data so the owner or user of a computer system cannot access it until a ransom is paid to the hackers who then unlock the data.

Government agencies, businesses, and consumers are struggling to protect themselves from cyber threats large and small.

Innovation in the form of stronger encryption has to move at unprecedented speed to try to catch up to the attacks currently being used.

In this fast-paced environment, businesses are offering some of the most important cybersecurity protections for digital communications.

The lessons that can be learned and the protections that could be developed is dependent on how well the private and public sectors cooperate.

I look forward to hearing from our witnesses on the issue of overstays.

Thank you.

Mr. RATCLIFFE. As I mentioned earlier, we are pleased to have with us a distinguished panel of witnesses today on this very important topic.

Mr. Matthew Eggers is the executive director of national security and preparedness at the U.S. Chamber of Commerce.

Good to have you back before our subcommittee, Matt.

Mr. Robert Mayer is the vice president of industry and State affairs at the U.S. Telecom Association.

We are glad to have you as well, Mr. Mayer.

Mr. Mark Clancy is the chief executive officer at Soltra.

Welcome, Mr. Clancy.

Mr. Mordecai Rosen is the general manager of the Security Business Unit at CA Technologies.

Thank you for being here today.

Finally, Ms. Ola Sage is the president and chief executive officer of e-Management.

Welcome, and again, welcome to you all. I would now like to ask the witnesses to stand and raise your right hand, so I can swear you in to testify.

[Witnesses sworn.]

Mr. RATCLIFFE. Let the record reflect that the witnesses answered in the affirmative. You all may be seated.

The witnesses' full statements will appear in the record. The Chair now recognizes Mr. Eggers, for 5 minutes, for his opening statement.

STATEMENT OF MATTHEW J. EGGERS, EXECUTIVE DIRECTOR, CYBERSECURITY POLICY, NATIONAL SECURITY AND EMERGENCY PREPAREDNESS, U.S. CHAMBER OF COMMERCE

Mr. EGGERS. Thank you, sir. Good morning, Chairman McCaul, Chairman Ratcliffe, Ranking Member Richmond, and other distinguished Members of the House Subcommittee on Cybersecurity, Infrastructure Protection, and Security Technologies.

My name is Matthew Eggers, and I am the executive director of cybersecurity policy with the U.S. Chamber. The chamber and I welcome the opportunity to testify.

I will confine my statements to CISA, or the Cybersecurity Information Sharing Act of 2015, which is Title I of the act that we are discussing today.

Last year, information-sharing legislation was the chamber's top cyber priority. We led the Protecting America's Cyber Networks Coalition, a partnership of more than 50 leading business associations representing nearly every sector of the U.S. economy.

CISA, a voluntary program, gives businesses legal certainty that they have safe harbor against frivolous lawsuits when freely sharing and receiving cyber threat data in real time.

CISA also offers protections related to public disclosure, regulatory and antitrust matters. The law safeguards individual's privacy and civil liberties. The chamber is championing CISA as part of our National cybersecurity campaign.

Businesses' use of CISA falls into roughly 4 categories. I am generalizing. One, earlier information-sharing leaders. Companies in this category are eager to see a sea change in the real-time sharing of threat indicators.

According to a chamber member who addressed the administration's cyber commission in May, our adversaries should only use an attack or technique once. If our business spots an attack today, all businesses should be protected against it by day's end.

This company and ones just like it is an active member of the sharing community. It wants public-private sharing capacity expanded right away. The chamber agrees.

No. 2, ISAO and ISAC members. Rank-and-file organizations in this group typically share cyber threat data with other businesses and with the Government through information-sharing bodies known as ISAOs and ISACs. This category is expected to swell as confidence in the CISA program grows and new information-sharing organizations are stood up. The administration's promotion of ISAOs is expected to have a positive influence, too.

No. 3, be intrigued, but cautious. I attended DHS's C3 program on June 1 in Indianapolis, and one individual's remark comes to mind. He said, "I have heard about CISA, but we are not ready as a company to participate. It will take a cultural shift." This person's apprehension tells us how central it is that trust in CISA's protection be earned and maintained.

No. 4, small businesses and under-resourced organizations. A goal of information-sharing legislation is to foster economies of scale in real-time sharing. The chamber believes that the market will eventually provide inexpensive and easy-to-use technologies that conform to CISA's rules and generate and swap indicators at internet speeds. Such an outcome is important for small and under-resourced organizations.

The chamber is a strong supporter of CISA, but it's not a silver-bullet solution. CISA is part of a mix of policies that need to advance together.

Some select examples. First, the joint-industry NIST cyber framework is a sound baseline for businesses' cybersecurity practices. The chamber urges policymakers to help agencies streamline existing regulations with the framework. We oppose the creation of new mandates.

Second, the chamber is engaging issues that are linked to information sharing. The chamber supports a piloting, a CIDAR, which is shorthand for a Cyber Incident Data and Analysis Repository. Also, we appreciate Congress' efforts to press the administration to renegotiate the Wassenaar Agreement control language governing so-called intrusion software. Industry is urging Wassenaar officials to eliminate the controls on technology software and hardware. Discussions are underway, but we still have much work to do.

The CISA program is off to a good start. CISA procedures and guidance were finalized yesterday, and chamber members will review them.

While oversight by Congress is crucial, it is too soon to make changes to the legislation. CISA does not need to be reauthorized for several years. The chamber's public message is two-fold. No. 1, to policymakers we say thank you for getting CISA done, and we urge lawmakers and the administration to be industry's ally as they use the program. No. 2, to businesses we say that you should use the framework, join an ISAO or an ISAC and take advantage of the CISA AIS system as appropriate.

The chamber believes that CISA will enable private organizations to be more secure and resilient against America's cyber adversaries.

Thank you for giving me the opportunity to convey the chamber's views. I am happy to answer any questions.

[The prepared statement of Mr. Eggers follows:]

PREPARED STATEMENT OF MATTHEW J. EGGERS

JUNE 15, 2016

Good morning, Chairman McCaul, Ranking Member Thompson, and other distinguished Members of the House Homeland Security Committee (committee). My name is Matthew Eggers, and I am the executive director of cybersecurity policy with the U.S. Chamber's National Security and Emergency Preparedness Department. On behalf of the chamber, I welcome the opportunity to testify before the committee regarding industry's perspectives on the Cybersecurity Act of 2015.

The chamber's National Security and Emergency Preparedness Department was established in 2003 to develop and implement the chamber's homeland and National security policies. The Department's Cybersecurity Working Group, which I lead, identifies current and emerging issues, crafts policies and positions, and provides analysis and direct advocacy to Government and business leaders.

The chamber applauds the committee and its staff members for their dedication to getting cybersecurity information-sharing legislation enacted. Recent cyber incidents in the public and private sectors underscore the need for legislation to help businesses improve their awareness of cyber threats and to enhance their protection and response capabilities in collaboration with Government entities. Cyber attacks aimed at businesses and Government bodies are increasingly being launched from sophisticated hackers, organized crime, and state-sponsored groups. These attacks are advancing in scope and complexity. Industry and Government have a mutual interest in bolstering the economic security of the U.S. business community.

CYBERSECURITY INFORMATION SHARING ACT OF 2015 (CISA): THE BASICS

I will largely confine my written statement to the Cybersecurity Information Sharing Act of 2015 (CISA), which is title I of the Cybersecurity Act of 2015.[1] President Obama signed this legislation into law in December 2015. The House passed two cybersecurity information-sharing bills in April 2015 with robust majorities from both parties and with broad industry backing. Indeed, the House's action prodded the full Senate to take up cybersecurity information-sharing legislation in the fall.

Passing cybersecurity information-sharing legislation was the top cyber policy priority of the chamber. We led the Protecting America's Cyber Networks Coalition (the coalition), a partnership of more than 50 leading business associations representing nearly every sector of the U.S. economy. It took a dedicated team working with Capitol Hill and the administration to get CISA done.

CISA establishes a voluntary information-sharing program, intended to strengthen businesses' protection and resilience against cyber attacks. The law gives businesses legal certainty that they have safe harbor against frivolous lawsuits when freely sharing and receiving cyber-threat indicators (CTIs) and defensive measures (DMs) in real time and taking actions to mitigate cyber attacks. CISA also offers protections related to public disclosure, regulatory, and antitrust matters in order to increase the timely exchange of information among public and private entities.

The law safeguards individuals' privacy and civil liberties and establishes appropriate roles for Government agencies and departments. CISA reflects sound compromises among many parties on these issues.[2]

---

[1] The cyber legislation was included in the Consolidated Appropriations Act, 2016 (Pub. L. No. 114–113). *www.congress.gov/bill/114th-congress/house-bill/2029.*

[2] See Automated Indicator Sharing (AIS) resources, including the Cybersecurity Information Sharing Act of 2015 (CISA) implementation procedures and guidance, available at *www.us-*

Continued

CISA called for the Department of Homeland Security (DHS) to establish a "capability and process" (aka a portal) in the Department to receive CTIs and DMs shared by businesses with the Federal Government in an electronic format—i.e., through email or media, an interactive form on an internet website, or a real-time, automated process. In March 2016, DHS launched an Automated Indicator Sharing (AIS) platform that enables the Government and the private sector to exchange cybersecurity threat information with one another.[3] The AIS initiative reportedly has more than 100 participants—spanning the banking, energy, and technology sectors, as well as both small and large companies—up from 6 participants this past spring.

Groups have begun testing their ability to share and receive indicators, but there is not yet sharing on a massive scale. The platform uses technical specifications, including the Trusted Automated eXchange of Indicator Information (TAXII), which defines a set of services and message exchanges that, when implemented, enable sharing of actionable cyber threat information. It also uses Structured Threat Information eXpression (STIX), a collaborative effort to develop a structured language to represent threat information.[4]

An industry participant at last week's (June 9) CISA implementation workshop captured the thinking of many when he said, "Our adversaries are employing automated techniques against us. Machine-to-machine sharing is a key element needed to help solve our cybersecurity problems." He added that the United States cannot succeed if we pit cyber professionals—which are a significantly limited workforce asset—against machines.

CHAMBER PROMOTING CISA AS PART OF OUR NATIONAL CYBER CAMPAIGN

The chamber is championing CISA as part of our National cybersecurity campaign. The chamber will develop a document in concert with industry groups and other parties, including DHS and the Department of Justice (DOJ), that summarizes the CISA/AIS program, describes participants' protections and obligations, and urges the private sector to get involved in the AIS network. Appropriate, real-time automated sharing will strengthen the security and resilience of industry and Government, thus heightening the costs of executing malicious attacks by U.S. adversaries. Many experts contend that the timely sharing of cyber indicators among various information-sharing and analysis organizations (ISAOs), information-sharing and analysis centers (ISACs), and private- and public-sector entities can reduce both the probability and the severity of cybersecurity incidents. (ISACs are considered to be ISAOs.)

The chamber launched our cybersecurity roundtable series in 2014. This National initiative recommends that businesses of all sizes and sectors adopt fundamental internet security practices, including using the framework and similar risk management tools, engaging cybersecurity providers, and partnering with law enforcement before cyber incidents occur. Nine regional roundtables and two summits in Washington, DC, have been held since 2014. More events are planned this year, including in San Antonio, Texas, on June 28 and in Chicago (Schaumburg, Illinois) on July 12. The chamber's Fifth Annual Cybersecurity Summit will be held on September 27.

Each regional event includes approximately 200 attendees and typically features cybersecurity principals from the White House, DHS, the National Institute of Standards and Technology (NIST), and local FBI and Secret Service officials.

CISA IMPLEMENTATION GUIDANCE AND PROCEDUERS: A GOOD START

The enactment of CISA triggered an array of Government guidelines and procedures. The chamber has tracked implementation dates and monitored agencies' progress toward meeting the deadlines—and DHS and the DOJ delivered.

---

cert.gov/ais. Also see pro-CISA advocacy papers: "It's About Protecting America's Cyber Networks, Not Surveilling You" (August 10, 2015) [http://www.uschamber.com/sites/default/files/cisa_myth_v_fact_cyber_protection_not_surveillance_final_0.pdf]; "Sharing Cyber Threat Indicators (CTIs)—Separating Fact From Fiction" (August 19, 2015) [http://www.uschamber.com/sites/default/files/cisa_ctis_separating_fact_from_fiction_aug_19-_final.pdf]; "'Voluntary' Means Voluntary—Separating Fact From Fiction" (August 26, 2015); and "Going on the 'Defensive'—Separating Fact From Fiction" (October 5, 2015) [http://www.uschamber.com/sites/default/files/cisa_going_on_the_defensive_separating_fact_-from_fiction_oct_5_final.pdf]. http://insidecybersecurity.com/daily-news/info-sharing-debate-shifts-implementation-privacy-advocates-now-back-cyber-law.

[3] www.us-cert.gov/ais.

[4] http://blogs.wsj.com/cio/2016/03/21/homeland-security-department-launches-cyber-threat-sharing-platform.

In particular, DHS and DOJ released interim guidance in February 2016 to assist "non-Federal entities"—including organizations in the private sector and State and local governments—to share CTIs with the Federal Government. The departments also released interim procedures relating to the receipt and use of CTIs by the Federal Government, interim guidelines relating to privacy and civil liberties in connection with the exchange of these indicators, and guidance to Federal agencies on sharing information in the Government's possession.

At the time of this writing, the chamber expects that DHS and DOJ officials will release by June 15 final procedures and guidance, which we generally agree with. We anticipate that the departments will accommodate the chamber's request to clarifying the protections afforded to a non-Federal entity when it shares cyber threat information with another non-Federal entity. The chamber and public authorities have a mutual interest in ensuring that the important protections authorized under CISA are clearly stated and utilized.

LOOKING AHEAD: PROMOTING CISA, BUILDING AND MAINTAING TRUST

Looking forward to the next several months, the chamber believes that businesses' use of the CISA program arguably falls into roughly 4 categories. I want to emphasize that these groups are generalizations—shorthand for where private entities are in the information-sharing ecosystem.

- *Early Information-Sharing Leaders: Increasing the Quality and Volume of Sharing Under CISA.*—Private organizations in this category are actively engaged in sharing threat data. They were in the vanguard of businesses establishing and funding ISAOs and ISACs several years ago. Companies in this grouping have long-established information-sharing relationships among multiple industry peers and Government partners, and several of them are already directly connected to sharing programs like AIS.[5]

  CISA should give the lawyers and risk management professionals in these top organizations added certainty to receive CTIs and DMs and to share them with business and the Government. A core purpose of the new law is to extend liability protections to companies to encourage them to share cyber threat information.[6]

  Companies in this category are eager to see a sea change in the real-time sharing of threat indicators within and across sectors, as well as between Government and businesses. According to a chamber member who addressed on May 16 the Commission on Enhancing National Cybersecurity, "Our adversaries should only use an attack or technique once. If our business spots an attack today, all businesses should be protected against it by day's end." Clearly, this company is an active member of the sharing community and wants public-private capacity to expand their capability to exchange threat data immediately. The chamber agrees.

- *ISAOs/ISACs Members: Leveraging the Expanding Network of Sharing Conduits.*—Many members in this dispersed network of ISAOs/ISACs do not share cybersecurity threat data directly with the Government. Instead, rank-and-file members in this category typically share CTIs and DMs with other businesses and with the Government through the channels that information bodies (e.g., the Financial Services–ISAC, the Oil and Natural Gas–ISAC) provide. This category is expected to swell as confidence in the CISA program grows and new information-sharing organizations are stood up over the coming months and years.

  The comparatively new ISAO standards organization is a key component of the Obama administration's cybersecurity strategy, launched in early 2015.[7] The administration's promotion of ISAOs is designed to encourage the protected sharing of information based on emerging and evolving threats that transcend

---

[5] *www.dhs.gov/topic/cybersecurity-information-sharing.*

[6] *http://insidecybersecurity.com/daily-news/mccaul-evaluate-effectiveness-cyber-info-sharing-law-including-liability-protections.*

[7] In February 2015, President Obama signed an Executive Order (EO) to promote cybersecurity information sharing among multiple business and Government entities. The EO urges the private sector to develop information sharing and analysis organizations (ISAOs) to serve as focal points for cybersecurity information sharing and collaboration within the private sector and between the private sector and Government. *www.whitehouse.gov/the-press-office/2015/02/13/executive-order-promoting-private-sector-cybersecurity-information-shari.*

industry sectors and geographic regions.[8] CISA is expected to have a positive influence on the expansion of the community of ISAOs and ISACs.

- *The Intrigued But Cautious: Sharing Should Pick Up as Both Education and Confidence Increase.*—Businesses in this category have probably heard something about CISA through social media, cybersecurity events, and colleagues. Business leaders are interested in protected sharing arrangements, yet they are not ready to commit to routine sharing and receiving. Perhaps they do not know how to begin. The former view is due to misgivings about CISA's protections. The latter situation can be addressed through outreach and education.

  Many cautious businesses have pictures in their heads of bureaucrats lying in wait with regulations and privacy groups readying law suits. The chamber does not agree completely with these perspectives, but we hear them expressed frequently. I attended a DHS-led C3 Voluntary Program in early June in Indianapolis and one individual's remark comes to mind. He said, "I have heard about CISA. But we are not ready as a company to participate—it will take a cultural shift." This person's apprehension tells us how central it is that trust in CISA's protections be earned and maintained. The chamber and most Government leaders appreciate that business attitudes change over time and participation in CISA/AIS will be gradual.

  One change that may accelerate the use of CISA is business contracting arrangements. The chamber foresees situations where large firms require their supply chain partners to belong to an ISAO/ISAC and to utilize AIS or some other automated means of timely indicator sharing.

- *Small Businesses and Underresourced Organizations: Indirect Beneficiaries of Innovations in Sharing.*—Many small and midsize businesses, especially underresourced enterprises, will be able to benefit from an innovative, automated sharing ecosystem. A key long-term goal of information-sharing legislation is to foster economies of scale in real-time sharing. The chamber anticipates that the marketplace will eventually provide inexpensive and easy-to-deploy technologies that conform to CISA's rules (e.g., scrubbing privacy information from CTIs) and generate and swap threat signatures at internet speeds. Systems like AIS will be able to block attacks sooner and more regularly, compared with the relatively human-intensive sharing schemes in use today.

CISA FITS WITHIN A COLLECTION OF POLICY ISSUES THAT NEED ATTENTION

The chamber is a strong supporter of CISA and its potential to clear away real or perceived hurdles to information sharing. CISA is not a silver-bullet solution to our Nation's cybersecurity challenges. However, chamber members say that increasing the speed and quality of bilateral information flows of CTIs and DMs is essential for developing a holistic approach to cyber defense. CISA is part of a mix of cybersecurity policies that need to advance together.

Here are some select issues that are worth highlighting for the committee:

First, the joint industry-NIST *Framework for Improving Critical Infrastructure Cybersecurity* (the framework) is a sound baseline for businesses' cybersecurity practices. The CISA program and the framework are highly complementary. Businesses implement a cybersecurity risk management program before investing in information-sharing programs. In February 2016, the chamber sent a letter to NIST, commenting on the framework.

Key points that the chamber made in the letter include the following:

- The chamber has been actively promoting the framework.
- Chamber members are using the framework and urging business partners to manage cybersecurity risks to their information networks and systems.
- The chamber urges policymakers to help agencies and departments with streamlining existing regulations with the framework and maintaining the framework's voluntary nature.
- Industry opposes the creation of new or quasi-cybersecurity regulations, particularly when Government authorities have not taken affected entities' perspectives into account.[9]

The bottom line: The chamber values the Obama administration's leadership on the non-regulatory framework and urges the next administration to actively support it. NIST did an admirable job working with industry to development the tool. As framework stakeholders begin the year-long transition from the Obama administra-

---

[8] *http://insidecybersecurity.com/daily-news/isao-standards-body-issue-next-round-draft-plans-info-sharing-july.*

[9] *http://csrc.nist.gov/cyberframework/rfi_comments_02_2016/20160209_US_Chamber_of_Commerce.pdf.*

tion to its successor, the chamber wants to sustain the view held by most businesses and policymakers that the framework is a policy and political cornerstone for managing enterprise cybersecurity risks and threats.

To sustain the momentum behind the framework, the chamber believes that both industry and government have jobs to do. On the one hand, the chamber has been actively promoting the framework since it was released in 2014. Our national cybersecurity campaign is funded through members' sponsorships and through the contributions of State and local chambers of commerce, other business organizations, and academic institutions. Further, chamber members are using the framework and urging business partners to manage cybersecurity risks to their data and devices. Industry is working with government entities, including DHS, to strengthen their information networks and systems against malicious actors.

On the other hand, the chamber urges policymakers to help agencies and departments with harmonizing existing regulations with the framework and maintaining the framework's voluntary nature. Our organization opposes the creation of new or quasi-cybersecurity regulations, especially when government authorities have not taken affected entities' perspectives into account.

Second, the chamber is engaging policy issues that ultimately relate to cybersecurity information sharing.

- The chamber supports piloting a CIDAR, shorthand for a cyber incident data and analysis repository. In May 2016, we sent a letter to DHS saying that (1) data submitted to a CIDAR need to be made anonymous, (2) additional sharing protections may be needed, and (3) an experimental CIDAR could offer tangible upsides to public- and private-sector cybersecurity. Comprehensive information about cyber events could assist insurers in expanding cyber coverage and in identifying cybersecurity best practices for their customers.
- The chamber appreciates the efforts of the Congressional Cybersecurity Caucus, particularly co-chairs McCaul and Langevin, to press the administration to renegotiate the Wassenaar Agreement (WA) control language governing so-called intrusion software and surveillance items aspects of a controversial international agreement to prevent the export of sophisticated hacking tools to repressive governments and criminal organizations.

Industry and democratic governments have a mutual interest in keeping malicious software out of the hands of bad actors. But the 2013 WA control language governing so-called intrusion software and surveillance items takes a seriously wrong approach to cybersecurity.[10]

WA officials are gathering from June 20 to 24 in Vienna, Austria, at the working-group level. Industry is urging officials to completely eliminate the controls on technology, software, and hardware. If deleting the controls is not possible, the chamber and many others recommend that WA officials substantially narrow the scope of the control language and dramatically simplify the language in order to bring clarity and enable compliance.[11] If the WA control language is not eliminated or at least adequately amended, it could have a powerfully (unintended) negative effect on the CISA program. Creating cybersecurity policies and laws in the WA environment lacks sufficient transparency and does not advance public-private partnerships at home and abroad.

- On June 8, the chamber's board of directors approved a policy statement on cybersecurity norms and deterrence. The paper argues that despite the existence of written blueprints, such as ones related to global prosperity and defense, the U.S. cybersecurity strategy is seemingly uncertain—both to many in the private sector and our adversaries alike. The chamber believes that policymakers need to refocus National and global efforts to heighten the costs on sophisticated attackers that would willfully hack America's private sector for illicit purposes. Public-private policymaking needs to spotlight increasing adherence to international norms and deterrence to reduce the benefits of conducting harmful cyber activity against the U.S. business community and the Nation. The statement makes several policy endorsements. For instance, the chamber contends that the United States and its allies should enhance businesses' situational awareness through protected information sharing.

---

[10] *https://www.uschamber.com/sites/default/files/documents/files/final_group_letter_-bis_proposed_rule_intrusion_software-surveillance_items_july_20_2015.pdf.*

[11] *http://insidecybersecurity.com/daily-news/obama-administration-agrees-renegotiate-cyber-export-controls.*

RECOMMENDATIONS ON CONGRESSIONAL OVERSIGHT

The chamber believes that the CISA program is off to a good start. The CISA/AIS implementation guidance documents will likely be finalized today. We look forward to reviewing them with our members. The chamber appreciates the open and constructive discussions that we have had with DHS and DOJ officials. While oversight by Congress is crucial, it is too soon to make changes to the legislation. CISA does not need to be reauthorized for several years (i.e., September 2025).

The chamber's public message is two-fold:

- To policymakers we say thank you for getting the cybersecurity information-sharing legislation across the finish line. And we urge lawmakers and the administration to be industry's ally as they use the program. Companies need to feel that policymakers have their backs. It is important that businesses see that the protections granted by the law-including matters tied to limited liability, regulation, antitrust, and public disclosure-become real.
- To businesses we say that you should use the framework, join an ISAO/ISAC, and take advantage of the CISA/AIS system as appropriate. The chamber urges the senior leaders of industry groups to promote these initiatives among their peers and constituencies.

The chamber and many stakeholders worked diligently over several years to craft policy that would serve multiple interests—namely individuals' security and privacy. We believe that CISA will enable private organizations of all sizes and sectors to be more secure and resilient against America's cyber adversaries.

Mr. RATCLIFFE. Thank you, Mr. Eggers.

The Chair now recognizes Mr. Mayer, for 5 minutes, for his opening statement.

STATEMENT OF ROBERT H. MAYER, VICE PRESIDENT, INDUSTRY AND STATE AFFAIRS, UNITED STATES TELECOM ASSOCIATION

Mr. MAYER. Thank you. Good morning, Chairman McCaul, Chairman Ratcliffe, Ranking Member Richmond, and distinguished Members of the committee.

My name is Robert Mayer, and I serve as vice president of industry and State affairs at the United States Telecom Association. Thank you for giving the communications sector and me personally the opportunity to appear before you today for this important oversight hearing.

Today, our Nation faces unrelenting assaults from a variety of bad actors, including, among others, nation-states, criminal enterprises, terror organizations and individual and group hackers. As new interconnected platforms, technologies, and applications grow exponentially, so does the attack surface expand, placing every U.S. citizen and organization in harm's way.

In this setting, information sharing represents a fundamental building block in protecting the vital interests of all well-intended stakeholders in the cyber ecosystem. The U.S. Congress and this committee in particular are to be applauded for passing bipartisan legislation that now serves as a cornerstone in protecting our Nation's economic and National security from the perils of cyber attack.

The Cybersecurity Act of 2015 is a complex bill that represents a careful balance of interests across a broad spectrum of stakeholders. The act was founded on the voluntary sharing of information and provides authority for preventing, detecting, analyzing, and mitigating cybersecurity threats.

On the privacy front, great care was taken to safeguard individuals from having their personal information shared with the Government in a manner not directly related to specifically authorized activities. Of great importance to our industry were the assurances that information shared with our Government partners would not be directly used to regulate lawful activity, to monitor or operate defensive measures, or share cybersecurity threat indicators.

Similarly, protections from Federal and State disclosure laws provide the appropriate balance between interest and transparency, and vital information sharing. Furthermore, by authorizing the EINSTEIN 3 Accelerated and Enhanced Cybersecurity Service programs and eliminating statutory obstacles to their implementation, the Act took important steps to make the network of Federal civilian agencies, State governments, critical infrastructure providers and other entities safer, especially from advanced, persistent threats.

Perhaps of greatest significance on the impact of future information sharing were the protections from liability incorporated into the act. While there may remain some lingering questions in this area that will be the subject of further clarification, the lack of such protections was one of the most serious impediments to sharing information.

The communication sector has been actively engaged in information sharing, operational and planning activities at DHS and elsewhere both before and subsequent to the passage of the act. Today at the operational level, over 50 private companies and 24 Federal agencies share critical communications information in the DHS National Coordination Center which also operates as our communications ISAC.

Another noteworthy undertaking in this area involves activity in the Communications Sector Coordinating Council where a new committee was created following the passage of the act to evaluate current information-sharing activities and what the sector can do to support new and evolving initiatives.

That committee is also planning to conduct a preliminary assessment of how the current, more narrowly circumscribed information sharing has been effectively and appropriately expanded as a consequence of the legislation adopted by Congress.

While the act is only 6 months old, it is already evident that the new law is having an impact on both industry and Government efforts to facilitate greater information sharing.

We want to take this opportunity to acknowledge the significant and largely successful efforts by DHS to meet their aggressive implementation and guidance deadlines. Both DHS and the DOJ have been extremely forthcoming with respect to explaining and clarifying administrative, operational, technical, and legal aspects associated with implementing information-sharing mechanisms, including those associated with a newly modified, automated information-sharing capability.

While there are still some operational improvements needed to facilitate the efficient sharing of both automated and non-automated processes, and Government guidelines remain to be finalized, there is clear evidence of a strong commitment on the part of industry and government to address any remaining barriers.

Several major companies in our sector are already enrolled in the program and others are in process of completing their evaluations.

One note of concern that we would like to share with this committee involves the implications of potential privacy rules that the FCC recently announced. Under the act, an entity can share information on a specific person if at the time of the sharing that entity did not knowingly reveal personal information unrelated to a cybersecurity threat.

Unlike the language in the act, the FCC proposal would grant the protection only when the sharing is shown to be, "reasonably necessary." This language creates ambiguity and uncertainty and is likely to spur reticence on the part of the companies, who could fear enforcement action based on an after-the-fact FCC determination of reasonableness. We will work hard to secure the appropriate clarity, and we continue to engage the FCC in this rulemaking proceeding.

In closing, let me once again thank the committee for their ongoing work to oversee the implementation of this landmark legislation. Given the magnitude of the threat and the promise of this legislation, periodic oversight by this committee will only bring us closer to making the cyber world much safer.

Thank you, and I look forward to your questions.

[The prepared statement of Mr. Mayer follows:]

PREPARED STATEMENT OF ROBERT H. MAYER

JUNE 15, 2016

Chairman McCaul, Ranking Member Thompson, and distinguished Members of the committee, thank you for giving the Communications Sector and me personally the opportunity to appear before you today for this important oversight hearing.

My name is Robert Mayer, and I serve as vice president of industry and state affairs at the United States Telecom Association. USTelecom represents companies ranging from some of the smallest rural broadband providers to some of the largest companies in the U.S. economy. I am a past chair and current cybersecurity committee chair of the Communications Sector Coordinating Council (CSCC) which represents the Broadcasting, Cable, Satellite, Wireless, and Wireline segments. The CSCC is one of the 16 critical infrastructure sectors under the Critical Infrastructure Partnership Advisory Council (CIPAC) through which the Department of Homeland Security (DHS) facilitates physical and cyber coordination and planning activities among the private sector and Federal, State, local, territorial, and Tribal governments.

Today, our Nation faces unrelenting assaults from a variety of bad actors including, among others, nation-states, criminal enterprises, terror organizations and individual and group hackers. And as new interconnected platforms, technologies and applications grow exponentially, so does the attack surface expand placing every U.S. citizen and organization in harm's way. In this setting, information sharing represents a fundamental building block in protecting the vital interests of all well-intended stakeholders in the cyber ecosystem.

The United States Congress and this committee in particular are to be applauded for passing bipartisan legislation that now serves as a cornerstone in protecting our Nation's economic and National security from the perils of a cyber attack. The Cybersecurity Act of 2015 is a complex bill that represents a careful balance of interests across a broad spectrum of stakeholders.[1] The Act is founded on the voluntary sharing of information and provides authority for preventing, detecting, analyzing, and mitigating cybersecurity threats and includes fundamental protections important to our industry including those related to privacy; exposure to regulation; State, Tribal, or local disclosure laws; and general legal liabilities.

On the privacy front, great care was taken to safeguard individuals from having their personal information shared with the Government in a manner not directly related to specifically authorized activities associated with cyber threat indicators and

---

[1] Cybersecurity Act of 2015 was passed as part of the Consolidated Appropriations Act, 2016, Pub. L. No. 114–113, 129 Stat. 2242 (available at *https://www.congress.gov/114/plaws/publ113/PLAW-114publ113.pdf*).

defensive measures. Of great importance to our industry were the assurances that information shared with our Government partners would not be directly used to regulate—including enforcement actions—lawful activity to monitor, operate defensive measures or share cyber threat indicators. Similarly, protections from Federal and State disclosure laws provide the appropriate balance between interests in transparency while not impeding vital information sharing.

Finally, by authorizing the EINSTEIN 3 Accelerated (E3A) and Enhanced Cybersecurity Service (ECS) programs, and eliminating statutory obstacles to their implementation, the Act took important steps to make the networks of Federal civilian agencies, State governments, critical infrastructure providers and other entities safer, especially from advanced persistent threats.

Perhaps of greatest significance on the impact of future information sharing were the protections from liability incorporated into the Act. While there may remain some lingering questions in this area that are now the subject of further clarification, the lack of such protections was one of the most serious impediments to sharing information. The law establishes an appropriate standard by applying an exemption to liability protection only in such instances where there was a knowing sharing of personal information or information that identifies a specific person not directly related to a cybersecurity threat or where there exists evidence of gross negligence or willful misconduct in the course of conducting the authorized activities.

The Communications Sector has been actively engaged in information sharing operational and planning activities at DHS and elsewhere, both before and subsequent to the passage of the Act. Today at the operational level, over 50 private-sector communications and information technology companies and 24 Federal Government agencies share critical communications information and advice in the DHS National Coordination Center (NCC) which also operates as the Communications Information Sharing and Analysis Center (ISAC) in accordance with a 2000 Presidential Directive.[2] In this trusted NCC/Comms ISAC environment, information on cyber vulnerabilities, threats, intrusion, and anomalies is routinely exchanged among Government and industry participants.[3]

Another noteworthy undertaking is this area involves activity in a newly-established information sharing committee under the CSCC. This committee was created following the passage the Act to evaluate current information-sharing activities and what the sector can do to support new and evolving initiatives. The committee has identified a variety of mechanisms and venues for information sharing including those with trusted peers and commercial partners, Government agencies under contract, law enforcement, industry peers as part of the sector policy and planning process, DHS via the National Cybersecurity and Communications Integration Center (NCCIC) and other affiliated organizations like US–CERT, other public and private partners and finally by ISPs for their own internal use to protect their networks and customers. The committee is also planning to conduct a preliminary assessment of how the current, more narrowly circumscribed information sharing has been effectively and appropriately expanded as a consequence of the legislation adopted by Congress.

While the Act is only 6 months old, it is already evident that this new law is having an impact on both industry and Government efforts to facilitate greater information sharing. We want to take this opportunity to acknowledge the significant and largely successful efforts by DHS to meet their aggressive implementation and guidance deadlines. Both DHS and the Department of Justice have been extremely forthcoming with respect to explaining and clarifying administrative, operational, technical, and legal aspects associated with implementing information sharing mechanisms including those associated with a newly modified, Automated Information Sharing (AIS) capability.[4] While there are still some operational improvements needed to facilitate the efficient sharing of both automated and non-automated processes, and Government guidelines remain to be finalized, there is clear evidence of a strong commitment on the part of industry and Government to address any remaining barriers. Several major companies in our sector are already enrolled in the program and others are in the process of completing their initial evaluations.

One note of concern that we would like to share with this committee involves the implications of potential privacy rules that the FCC announced in their recent No-

---

[2] Presidential Policy Directive 63, (available at *http://fas.org/irp/offdocs/pdd/pdd-63.htm*).
[3] See, DHS description of the NCC/Comms ISAC (available at *www.dhs.gov/national-coordinating-center-communications*).
[4] See DHS information on Automated Information Sharing Program (available at *https://www.dhs.gov/ais*).

tice of Proposed Rulemaking.[5] Under the Act, an entity can share information on a specific person if at the time of the sharing that entity did not knowingly reveal personal information unrelated to a cybersecurity threat.[6] Unlike the language in the Act that would allow for liability protection in such instances, the FCC proposal would grant the protection only when the sharing is shown to be "reasonably necessary."[7] This language creates ambiguity and uncertainty and is likely to spur reticence on the part of companies who could fear enforcement action based on an after-the-fact FCC determination of reasonableness. We will work hard to secure the appropriate clarity as we continue to engage the FCC in this rulemaking proceeding.

In closing, let me once again thank this committee for their on-going work to oversee the implementation of this landmark legislation. Given the magnitude of the threat and the promise of this legislation, periodic oversight by this committee will only bring us closer to making the cyber world much safer.

Mr. RATCLIFFE. Thank you, Mr. Mayer.

The Chair now recognizes Mr. Clancy, for 5 minutes, for his opening statement.

STATEMENT OF MARK G. CLANCY, CHIEF EXECUTIVE OFFICER, SOLTRA

Mr. CLANCY. Chairman McCaul, Chairman Ratcliffe and Ranking Member Richmond, and Members of this committee, thank you for scheduling today's hearing.

My name is Mark Clancy, and I am the chief executive officer of Soltra.

I want to thank you for your efforts and long-standing dedication to addressing cybersecurity concerns in this committee, including the passage of the cyber information-sharing legislation. CISA's passage was a critical step toward improving the collective resiliency of our Nation's critical infrastructure.

It has only been 6 months since CISA was signed into law, but its implementation is moving forward quickly. As an early participant in the DHS Automated Indicator Sharing System, I believe that Soltra can offer a unique window into AIS's progress, key lessons learned and suggested improvements as this implementation continues.

Formed in 2014, as a joint venture between DTCC and the FS–ISAC Act, Soltra and its automation software, Soltra Edge, are bringing cutting-edge innovation and technical capabilities to the cybersecurity information-sharing process. DTCC is a participant-owned and -governed cooperative that serves as critical infrastructure of the U.S. capital markets, as well as financial markets globally.

In 2015, DTCC subsidiaries processed securities transactions valued at $1.5 quadrillion. The FS–ISAC is a not-for-profit organization formed in 1999 to address cyber threats in the Nation's critical infrastructure. The FS–ISAC has grown rapidly in recent years, and today the FS–ISAC has nearly 7,000 member organizations across 37 countries.

Soltra leverages the unique expertise of both these entities in our solutions to shorten the time from awareness, to decision, to action in addressing cyber threats. Soltra began as a cross-industry initiative that provides a no-cost platform that users can access to share

---

[5] *Protecting the Privacy of Customers of Broadband and Other Telecommunications Services,* WC Docket No. 16–106, Notice of Proposed Rulemaking, FCC 16–39 (rel. Apr. 1, 2016) (FCC NPRM).
[6] See, Cybersecurity Act of 2015 Section 104(d)(2)(A).
[7] See, FCC NPRM at para. 117.

cyber threat intelligence, or CTI, within or across communities. After less than 18 months, Soltra Edge has been downloaded by over 2,600 organizations in 75 countries across 25 industries.

Our threat-sharing ecosystem relies on 3 open standards first developed by DHS and MITRE and now managed by OASIS. These are known as STIX, TAXII, and CYBEX. By using these standards, Soltra enables users to communicate CTI in a format that a human can understand and a machine can process, thereby cutting down hundreds of hours of effort that are currently needed to distill this information.

These open standards also allow Soltra users to exchange CTI from community sources like ISACs and ISAOs, commercial sources, Government sources such as DHS, Treasury, FBI, and utilize that information in a variety of commercial and open-source tools.

As I mentioned earlier, Soltra is one of the handful of companies that has already enrolled in AIS. DHS has been a helpful partner in this process, and as is normal in the case of any program there are a few areas that would benefit from clarification.

First and foremost, it has been our observation that additional guidance is needed from DHS and DOJ that the liability of protections under CISA cover private-to-private sharing. The initial guidance was silent on that point and created much confusion in the industry as a result.

Just as of today, it looks like that was addressed in the updated guidance that DHS had published, and we look forward to reviewing that in the fall.

As you know, privacy is and always will be a top priority for the financial services sector. As we move forward with CISA, additional guidance is also needed from DHS to provide clarity on the definition of personally identifiable information, or PII. Thus far, the definition of PII in the AIS guidance differs from the definition of PII in other DHS programs. It is critical that clarity be provided quickly by DHS to ensure top protections by all who participate in the program.

While it is still early on in the AIS program, I would like to focus on 5 recommendations for improving the AIS system. First, to maximize the potential of AIS, it would be beneficial to streamline the process for signing up and to simplify the process for obtaining digital certificates from Federal Bridge providers.

Second, various aspects of the law as well as the implementation have caused DHS to add extensions into the STIX standard. AIS also includes a series of required fields in STIX data submitted to the Department, which if not included will reject any attempted submission from a company. It would be helpful for DHS to specify those things up-front in order to help implementers understand what needs to be done in advance of connecting to the AIS system.

Third, DHS should issue guidance on how the CISCP program fits under CISA to provide greater verification.

Fourth, for greater participation and ease of use in the future, it would be beneficial to add a test environment where companies can ensure its AIS interface works effectively.

Finally, there are 3 main data points that the private sector would like to see added to the AIS system to help increase the effectiveness of the platform. These include additional information about the types of threat actors associated with threat intelligence, recommended defensive measures, and a feedback loop to refine the context of CTI data.

I want to thank you once again for providing me with the opportunity to share my insight today, and I look forward to working with the committee, Congress and the Executive branch as well as with our private-sector partners to achieve the collective goals of CISA. I would be happy to answer any questions that you may have.

[The prepared statement of Mr. Clancy follows:]

PREPARED STATEMENT OF MARK G. CLANCY

JUNE 15, 2016

Chairman Ratcliffe, Ranking Member Richmond, and Members of the committee, thank you for scheduling today's hearing on industry perspectives on the Cybersecurity Act of 2015 (CISA). My name is Mark Clancy, and I am the chief executive officer of Soltra. Soltra's mission is to design and deliver solutions that shorten the time from awareness, to decision to action, in addressing cyber threats.

First, thank you for all of your efforts and dedication to addressing key cybersecurity concerns and for successfully passing cybersecurity information-sharing legislation. As our Nation continues to confront serious cybersecurity threats to our critical infrastructure, cybersecurity information sharing is one critical way to address these challenges.

CYBERSECURITY INFORMATION SHARING

Cybersecurity information sharing has been a cornerstone of various aspects of my career, beginning in 2004. At that time, I was running Citigroup's global Security Incident Response Team. Twelve years ago, we worked to combat the menace of phishing attacks targeting our customers. We quickly learned that the criminals were using the same approaches to target customers of other financial institutions; and by bi-directional sharing of the technical observations of those attacks with our competitors, we all were better able to minimize the impacts of these incidents. That first generation model of sharing was born out of personal trust between individual practitioners who met face-to-face frequently.

By 2008, a new sharing model was needed as the Financial Services Information Sharing and Analysis Center (FS–ISAC) started to grow significantly. This second generation trust model had widened to a larger number of institutions and individuals who still meet face-to-face on occasion, but now had moved to using electronic mail lists as the primary method of exchanging information between face-to-face meetings.

By 2010, when I was the chief information security office at The Depository Trust and Clearing Corporation (DTCC), we realized the scale of the community and the tonnage of information being shared grew to the point we could not utilize all the information, and that a third generation approach to sharing was required to use standardization and automation. This lead to us exploring standards that described a cyber threat in such a way that a human could understand it, but a machine could process it.

SOLTRA CREATION: DTCC AND THE FS–ISAC COLLABORATION

Soltra is the financial industry's answer to the third-generation information-sharing model. Soltra is a joint venture created by DTCC and the FS–ISAC that leverages the unique expertise of both entities, bringing together the best and brightest of the industry.

DTCC is a participant-owned and governed cooperative that serves as the critical infrastructure for the U.S. capital markets as well as financial markets globally. At its core, it develops and harnesses technology to provide a variety of risk management and data services to the financial services industry. More than 40 years ago the firm was created largely out of the need to leverage technology and automation in order to ensure securities transactions were more efficiently settled, thereby reducing risk of loss in the event of a counterparty default. In this respect, DTCC presently is among the most sophisticated financial technology or "FinTech" companies.

Today, DTCC continues to deploy evolving and improving technology in service to its mission as the primary financial market infrastructure for the securities industry. DTCC simplifies the complexities of clearing, settlement, asset servicing, data management and information services across multiple asset classes. In 2014, DTCC's subsidiaries processed securities transactions valued at approximately US$1.6 quadrillion.

The FS–ISAC is a 501(c)6 nonprofit organization and is funded entirely by its nearly 7,000 member firms and sponsors. It was formed in 1999 in response to 1998 Presidential Decision Directive 63 (PDD 63), which called for the public and private sectors to work together to address cyber threats to the Nation's critical infrastructures. The FS–ISAC expanded its role to encompass physical threats after the attacks on 9/11/2001, and in response to Homeland Security Presidential Directive (HSPD) 7 (and its 2013 successor, Presidential Policy Directive (PPD) 21) and the Homeland Security Act.

The FS–ISAC has grown rapidly in recent years. In 2004, there were only 68 members which were mostly large financial services firms. Today, FS–ISAC has nearly 7,000 member organizations, including commercial banks and credit unions of all sizes; markets and equities firms; brokerage firms; insurance companies; payments processors; and 40 trade associations representing all of the U.S. financial services sector. Because today's cyber-criminal activities transcend country borders, the FS–ISAC has expanded globally and has active members in over 37 countries.

SOLTRA

Soltra advances cybersecurity capabilities and increases resilience of critical infrastructure organizations by collecting and distilling cybersecurity threat intelligence from a myriad of sources to help safeguard against cyber attacks and deliver automated services at "computer speed," cutting down the hundreds of human hours that are currently needed to distill cyber threat information.

Soltra began as a true cross-industry initiative that included a live prototype involving over 125 security practitioners that included FS–ISAC members, private-sector representatives from other critical sectors, and Government entities to refine the requirements, architecture, and design of Soltra's automation software, which is known as Soltra Edge.™ Soltra Edge provides for a free platform that users can access, and after less than a year-and-a-half, Soltra Edge has been downloaded by over 2,600 organizations in 75 countries spanning 25 industries to consume, utilize, and share cyber threat intelligence using open standards.

The Soltra Edge platform sends, receives, and stores messages of Cyber Threat Intelligence (CTI) in a standardized way. It hides the complexity of the underlying technical specification so that end users can setup and start receiving threat information in under 15 minutes in most cases, changing the paradigm where it could take months or millions of dollars to change internal systems if companies wanted to do it on its own. The information that is received can be used to push instructions to other security tools to perform detection and mitigation of those threats. To support the widest possible adoption, we also made a highly functional version of the platform available at no cost to end-user organizations to defend themselves. We also offer a low-cost or no-cost solution to ISAC and ISAO community organizations to act as the community hub for machine-to-machine threat sharing if they lack an existing operational capability. For organizations with additional needs, we also offer a paid membership which includes system integrations for platforms that have not adopted standards, enterprise grade operational features, and technical support.

SOLTRA CREATES THE FIRST-EVER INTEROPERABLE INFORMATION SHARING PLATFORM: PROVIDES CROSS-SECTOR SHARING TO BETTER COMBAT THREATS

Soltra has built a threat-sharing ecosystem using 3 open standards first developed by DHS and MITRE called the Structured Threat Information eXpression (STIX) and the Trusted Automated eXchange of Indicator Information (TAXII), and the Cyber Observable eXpression (CybOX). STIX, TAXII, and CybOX have been transitioned into an international standards body, OASIS. These open standards are foundational for the interoperability and machine processing that are key to addressing complexity, and acting on information quickly. The OASIS CTI Technical Committee, which maintain these standards, has the largest amount of corporate and individual members of any technical committee in the standards body.

Soltra utilizes these open standards and has the unique ability to be the "glue" between different sectors and to provide connectivity for those who do not have the time or infrastructure to manage the transition to STIX/TAXII. This common standard also allows a defender of networks to use CTI from community sources like ISACs and ISAOs; Government sources such as the U.S. Departments of Homeland

Security (DHS) and Treasury, along with the Federal Bureau of Investigation (FBI); and utilize that information in a variety of commercial and open-source security tools. It also addresses the problems companies currently have when using multiple vendors whose bundling of CTIs may only work with that same vendor's tools. Soltra fixes this problem and allows for the use and scalability of information from multiple sources to be utilized in multiple tools that detect or defend the network.

Soltra also helps break down barriers between and amongst key sectors of the economy, providing the bridge from financial services to key sectors like health, energy, retail, as well as State, local, Tribal, and territorial (SLTT) governments. Historically, sectors only shared information within that sector. While important and effective to do, it also stovepipes the fact that the attackers are using the same Tactics, Techniques, and Procedures (TTPs) against all sectors and allows them to effectively use the same tool to attack all sectors. Soltra breaks down the barriers to sharing by ultimately providing the "utility platform" and enabling interchange of, information already in the STIX/TAXII format. We see this today with firms that are members of multiple ISAC/ISAO organizations and with ISACs that have sharing relationships with each other. Both of these act as cross-sector bridges since it is simple to share information. Friction is greatly reduced when using Soltra to connect organizations—the same standard format, communications method, and access controls are used to respond to the data-handling instructions driven from the Traffic Light Protocol markings of content.

SOLTRA AND INFORMATION SHARING BRING GREATER SECURITY

Sharing information about threats remains essential as Mandiant reports[1] that for 2015 the median number of days from compromise to discovery was 146 days. This improved from a median of 229 days from the 2014 Mandiant report,[2] but is still an extensive window. The 47% of firms that detected a breach themselves took 56 days to discover the breach, but the 53% of firms notified by an external party had a median of 320 days from compromise to detection.

This is directly relevant to information sharing in two ways. First, the delta between the time of an internal and external notification are likely a symptom of poor access to information about threats or ability to act on that information. Second, information shared about threats may represent intrusion sets recently identified that had been in situ for a long time. We need to both increase the percentage of internally discovered breaches and shorten the time to detect them. Sharing CTI data is one such way these discoveries are made and timely sharing leads to timely discovery. Soltra is working to solve this problem by widening the access to CTI data and shortening the time to act on it over manual methods. It is hard to know with certainty why the industry improved the lag in compromise to discovery, but it is highly likely information sharing tipping defenders on what to look for was a part of the improvement.

Third, there are some important lessons learned about the benefits of sharing information that, quite simply, will vary based upon the maturity of the institution participating in the program. However, a few things are universal:

First, initially when a company receives CTI data, it is purely a consumer of that information. It might find that it has limited technical or operational capabilities to utilize some or all of the information in an effective way. For example, it may receive indicator information about malware on endpoint, but not have a capability to scan end points for such files. At that juncture, the company will begin to realize that it needs to better understand what is in the data to actually be able to utilize it. For example, understanding how to use information when the temporal context is of an intrusion 300 days ago is important. If it then looks for that activity from the moment the CTI is received, it could miss the event that precipitated the intrusion several hundred days earlier. If it was just recently reported, the original victim may have just identified it and that data, even if it is a year old, might be the clue needed to ascertain if the same incident had occurred in your infrastructure. As a company moves up the maturity curve, it also moves from primarily utilizing the telemetry which is represented by the CTIs and starts to utilize insights and contextual information to anticipate hazards down the road. Even in mature sectors the bulk of the activity is around the telemetry CTI data.

As a company matures into using CTI data that was shared, it starts to realize that some data lacks sufficient context and may appear to be a false positive. This comes about between the very natural tension between sharing quickly when information is fresh, but could still be incomplete. This also occurs by the very nature

---

[1] https://www2.fireeye.com/rs/848-DID-242/images/Mtrends2016.pdf.
[2] http://dl.mandiant.com/EE/library/WP_M-Trends2014_140409.pdf.

of the investigative process that produces information and observations of activity that may have occurred during an attack but could be unrelated to the attacker's actions and are an artifact of normal IT system behavior. In order to address this, a company will want to have a method to ask the producing source to confirm details, or perhaps after its own research it will understand the context was lost or the CTI data is, in fact, inaccurate. A company will need to have a mechanism to share these results back to the producing source so they can adjust the content and send out a revision to the community.

This is important to note because as a company builds information-sharing products it will need to support a range of needs and maturity levels. It will also need to have the capability to receive feedback on existing products in addition to the ability to consume new submissions from the community. Finally, a company will also need to create methods to address the level of trust needed between members of a community as that community scales and the parties become more remote to each other.

CISA IMPLEMENTATION

It has only been 6 months since CISA was signed into law, and while there has been a rapid fire of activity in that time, more work certainly remains to be done. Guidance issued on how to submit information under CISA by DHS/DOJ adhered to the letter of the law and described private-to-Government sharing, but was silent on private-to-private sharing. This created some confusion concerning the scope of liability or when protections might apply. As an example, the FS–ISAC had to send a memo to all its members to clarify that the protection in the law did apply to private-to-private communications within the FS–ISAC membership. As recently as Thursday, June 9, 2016, DHS advised that CISA covers private-to-private sharing and that it would be included in the revised guidance required by Congress on June 15, 2016.

Soltra is one of the handful of companies that already has enrolled to DHS's Automated Indicator Sharing (AIS) program. As required by law, in March 2016 DHS opened access to its AIS platform along with the procedural documents of how to submit data to comply with the requirement in the law related to personal information. DHS has been a helpful partner in this process, and as is normally the case in any program, there are a number of areas that would benefit from clarification at this juncture. They include:

1. Additional guidance is needed from DHS on the definition of Personally Identifiable Information (PII).—Thus far, the definition of PII in the AIS submission guidance differs from the definition of PII in other DHS programs and was not defined in the Act. The vast majority of information sharing about cyber threats does not involve any personal information, but the lack of clarity as to which definition would be used for personal information across DHS programs needs to be made clear. The financial sector sent a letter on May 11, 2016 to DHS and the U.S. Department of Justice (DOJ) asking for clarification on this matter.

2. Current "Lessons Learned" Using the AIS System: Streamline the process for signing up for AIS.—To enroll in the AIS program participants need to execute two agreements with DHS, enroll to get an authentication certificate from an approved FedBRIDGE provider, submit network address information, and technical details of the sharing platform to be used.

- *Digital Certificates.*—The AIS process requires all users to obtain a digital certificate from 1 of the 3 FedBRIDGE providers which has become a cumbersome process. As background, these certificates are traditionally issued to individuals to support strong authentication and email encryption whereas the use case for AIS is to authenticate a machine used for sharing within a company. At this juncture, the AIS system requires a single person within the company to obtain the certificate which then has to be loaded into the server to communicate with the AIS system. That automated process actually requires paper documentation that has to be sent to DHS via the U.S. mail system. While the need for the authentication is critical, there is an inherent disconnect between the ultimate goal of the AIS system which is machine-to-machine. Going forward, it would be more helpful for a system to be created that allows for an organization level credential to be issued to the server used by the company to participate in the program. Other submission methods such as the web form and fax do not have the same authentication requirements.
- *AIS Changes to STIX/TAXII Fields.*—Various aspects of the law as well as implementation have caused DHS to modify aspects of the STIX/TAXII fields. AIS also includes a series of "required" fields in STIX data submitted to the

department which if not included, will reject any attempted submission from a company. It would be helpful for DHS to specify those up-front in order to help companies understand what needs to be done in advance of connecting to the AIS system.

- *Clarify how CISA protections apply to CISCP.*—The AIS program does not support submissions of Proprietary Information (PROPIN) nor Protected Critical Infrastructure Information (PCII) although DHS does indicate information submitted under the CISCP program can receive protections for PROPIN or PCII. Many companies are used to submitting both PROPIN and PCII related information and it would be critical to ensure that companies can continue to do so, hopefully using the AIS system for sake of ease. DHS should also issue guidance on how the CISCP program fits under CISA to provide for greater clarifications.
- *Add a Test Environment Where Companies Can Ensure Its AIS Interface Works Effectively.*—As is the case with many systems, it is preferable to be able to test whether or not a company's systems are interoperable with the AIS platform. Short deadlines in the law required the AIS system to be stood up quickly, and at this point, DHS does not have a system integration or test environment available. As a result, a company must attempt to work out the various issues in a live production environment. Moving forward, a test environment would be helpful for other companies and may allow for greater participation and ease of use in the future.

NEW DATA POINTS TO ADD TO AIS

There are 3 main data points that the private sector would like to see added to the AIS system to help increase the effectiveness of the AIS system:

1. Types of Threat Actors.—It would be exceptionally helpful if the AIS data could include an assessment of the type of threat actor behind the activity when that is known. It is clear that there are practical challenges of "naming names" in an Unclassified context. However, examples exist, including in the 2013 Defense Science Board report, "Resilient Military Systems and the Advanced Cyber Threat,"[3] that includes a 6-tier scale that would provide sufficient context to companies without naming specific actors.

2. Defensive Measures.—One of CISA's objectives was to support the development of "defensive measures." While more work will be needed to get to that point, AIS could add in recommendations to how recipients might use the AIS data sets. For example if a set of AIS information was to include the suggested defensive measure of "block, mitigate, or monitor" it would inform consumers the best type of "defensive measure" to employee even if detailed recommendations are unavailable. This would be an important benefit to the AIS system that could bring a greater number of participants into the system.

3. Feedback Loop and Context to Data

Context is important for all companies who participate in the AIS program. As the AIS system continues to be fine-tuned, there are a number of issues that would be helpful to review and clarify which may increase greater connectivity and participation overall. As we know, the spectrum of possible participants will bring with them different skills, capabilities, and maturities so for those submitting to AIS the downstream recipients want to understand the context and credibility of the information from AIS. These types of questions are foundational issues that have come from the variety of sectors Soltra supports, including those that are participating in the AIS program or those who have indicated they intend to participate in the near future. In the near future, industry participants will want to be able to select the type of data they want to receive from AIS which could include sector-specific or even cross-sector information. Levels of "trust" associated with the data will be important and industry participants will want to understand what process DHS will use if AIS members ask for more specific information from the AIS system, including the ability for DHS to reach back out to the original submitter of the data. Ultimately, DHS will need to be able to communicate how its internal process is set up to identify and vet the data submitted, a challenge that many ISACs have gone through themselves. The DHS guidance does mention a process that will be put in place to deal with false positives and mechanisms to address updating data and it will be critical that DHS provide clarity on that quickly.

---

[3] *http://www.acq.osd.mil/dsb/reports/ResilientMilitarySystems.CyberThreat.pdf.*

CYBERSECURITY INFORMATION SHARING AND COLLABORATION PROGRAM (CISCP) AND
PRIVATE-SECTOR SECURITY CLEARANCES UNDER CISCP

Many of Soltra's customers and community members participate in the CISCP program, which is widely viewed as a beneficial program that facilitates cross-sector engagement with government. It brings private-sector and government analysts together at quarterly in-person meetings, the Advanced Technical Threat Exchanges (ATTE). CISCP also allows the private sector to work on the National Cybersecurity and Communications Integration Center (NCCIC) floor, giving participants access to DHS, LE, and IC analysts. We are seeing an increase in production around CISCP analysts turning FS–ISAC reports into CISCP Indicator Bulletins.

CHANGES TO SECURITY CLEARANCES NEEDED

Challenges continue to exist in obtaining security clearances for companies. First, post the cybersecurity attack on the Office of Personnel Management (OPM), clearance times are much longer.

Second, it would be helpful if there was more transparency into the process with key performance metrics being available to Critical Infrastructure and Key Resources (CIKR) members or their ISACs. It should include monthly breakdowns by sector and clearance types of the number of new clearances requested, the number of investigation completed, the aging of applications by stage, the number of reinvestigations initiated/completed per month, as well as median times for each stage.

Third, there have been a number of changes to the security clearance program that has caused a number of challenges to many companies, including those who have historically had individuals on the NCCIC floor. As background, private-sector companies have 2 routes to have essential personnel cleared for access to Classified Information. The first is the Private-Sector Clearance Program (PSCP) initiated via the sector-specific agency and sponsored/operated by DHS, and which holds clearances to the Secret level. The second route is by executing a Cooperative Research and Development Agreement (CRADA) with DHS. With a CRADA in place the firm needs to have a Facilities Clearance (FCL), which allows it to hold staff clearances up to Top Secret and have access to the NCCIC floor.

A recent change that greatly impacted a number of ISACs was the requirement to have the FCL in place for their company. This was not a previously requirement of the CRADA process for CISCP as DHS rolled it out and was added at later date by the Defense Security Service (DSS.) A number of ISACs did not have FCLs current and therefore were removed from the NCCIC floor leaving no representation in the coordination process for those sectors. These ISACs do not have Classified work areas in their offices and were using the NCCIC floor for any handling of Classified materials. The requirements for obtaining the FCL are determined by the DSS. One attribute of this process is a requirement to clear top executives or board directors for companies. This program requirement made a lot of sense in the Defense Sector when the main objective of the FCL was managing contractors working on defense system projects. With the cybersecurity threat, the majority of the attack surface is in the private sector and many of the companies are multinationals with non-U.S. citizens on corporate boards or executive management, rendering the existing scheme less tailored for successful application to today's environment.

The CISCP program with DHS requires a CRADA be in place for the receipt of Unclassified information such as Cyber Threat Indicators. As a direct result of the change requiring the FCL for the CISCP CRADA a number of financial sector firms are in the process of ending their CRADA with DHS and going back to using the PSCP program to avoid the entanglement of having top executives or board members without cybersecurity responsibilities having to hold clearances which are orthogonal to their duties for the company. Again this is to receive Unclassified information from the DHS CISCP program.

The ISAC's that have an FCL will participate in CISCP via the CRADA and then be able to share Unclassified information from CISCP with their members. As a practical matter, when Classified information is shared with the private sector, this is done in a U.S. Government Facility with the appropriate FCL in place. It is unclear how ISACs that do not have the FCL will participate in the CISCP program going forward.

In addition to the problems with the CRADA and FCL, the problems and frustration with the clearance processes remain.

NEXT STEPS

Implementation of the Cybersecurity Information Sharing Act is moving forward quickly and DHS, DOJ, and the Congress are to be commended for how quickly the

AIS system has been stood up, and the various guidance documents issued on time. As with every system, there are lessons learned and items that can be improved, and we look forward to working closely with DHS and others to achieve our collective goal.

Soltra and Soltra Edge are bringing cutting-edge innovation and technical capabilities to the cybersecurity information-sharing process. Soltra Edge is providing a simple and easy solution by providing the core backbone and technical processes that have previously prohibited many companies from sharing, thinking that the process is too cumbersome or difficult just to get started. Soltra is helping companies in all sectors to increase the ability and likelihood that information sharing can help provide vastly improved cybersecurity defenses and ultimately make it harder and more expensive for attackers. We look forward to working with this committee, Congress, and the Executive branch, as well as with all of our private-sector partners to achieve our collective goals.

Mr. RATCLIFFE. Thank you, Mr. Clancy.

The Chair now recognizes Mr. Rosen, for 5 minutes.

STATEMENT OF MORDECAI ROSEN, GENERAL MANAGER, SECURITY BUSINESS UNIT, CA TECHNOLOGIES

Mr. ROSEN. Good morning, Chairman McCaul, Chairman Ratcliffe, Ranking Member Richmond, and Members of the subcommittee. Thank you for the opportunity to appear before you today.

My name is Mordecai Rosen and I serve as the senior vice president and general manager of the Cybersecurity Business Unit at CA Technologies. CA is one of the largest enterprise software companies in the world. We serve a global customer base in nearly every major commercial and industrial sector. CA software helps our customers develop, manage and secure the systems and services that form the basis for the new application economy.

I want to thank the committee for getting the cybersecurity act of 2015 over the finish line last year. CA was a strong supporter of the legislation and is encouraged by DHS's implementation thus far.

I want to focus on two topics today. First, I plan to highlight why identity and access management are so important in protecting our infrastructure and establishing trust in the cybersecurity ecosystem. Second, I will provide our overall perspective on the act and its implementation.

Applications have become the central way businesses connect with their customers. Identity is the new security perimeter for the application economy. In virtually every large network breach in recent memory, compromised identities were the common threat.

CA believes that robust identity solutions covering both human-to-machine and machine-to-machine connections will be vital to protecting Government and commercial networks and applications. Identity solutions ensure that users, devices, and applications are who and what they say they are.

I want to congratulate DHS for the job they have done to date on implementation. The legislation had very aggressive time lines to get the program up and running. DHS has met those deadlines and has worked collaboratively with their Government and industry partners to provide clarity around the overall program, and this should be commended.

At the same time, there are specific areas where further clarification will help accelerate adoption. CA, like many organizations, is actively exploring participation in the DHS Automated Indicator Sharing program. While we have strong interest, we and others still have outstanding questions.

First, organizations will need even greater clarity on targeted liability protection for the database, shared or received. Our hope is that the updated guidance, which I know has been released this morning, that DHS releases will answer outstanding questions. DHS will need to remain actively engaged with industry to help them fully understand these protections.

Second, ensuring trust in the system and providing robust privacy protections will remain central to successful implementation and adoption. DHS must be able to effectively authenticate users that share or receive information under the program. For example, DHS must be able to confirm that a participant sharing information is a real entity, not a front for hackers.

We are concerned that confidence in the program will lessen if participants cannot be authenticated and the data being shared cannot be trusted. Maintaining confidence in the act's privacy protections remain critical. DHS's initial guidance made strong privacy commitments, but participants will need even greater clarity. Stakeholder outreach and engagement through implementation will ensure that privacy considerations remain at the forefront.

Third, we have to make it as easy as possible for organizations to participate. The uptake of automated, real-time information exchanges that protect user privacy will define whether the act is a success, and the data received must be timely and actionable for the program to have maximum impact.

We look forward to reviewing DHS's updated guidance and hope it will give us the certainty needed to become an active partner in the program.

You asked CA to also address the Federal agency cyber provisions contained in Title II of the act. The EINSTEIN and Continuous Diagnostics and Mitigation, CDM, programs, when fully deployed will help Government agencies be more secure. CA has been an active participant in Phase 2 of CDM, which addresses identity and access issues with a significant focus on privileged users.

Managing the rights of privileged users remains one of the most important areas of IT risk for organizations today. Improper actions by privileged users can have disastrous effects on IT operations and security. Privileged axis management solutions provide the visibility, monitoring, and control needed for users and accounts that have the keys to the kingdom.

Deployment of CDM is at a critical stage. We have growing concerns that this deployment will be delayed, however, because agencies do not have the adequate contracting personnel to acquire the services from DHS. We recommend the committee keep a watchful eye on this issue as part of your oversight.

Thank you for your focus on cyber threat information sharing. CA stands ready to continue our partnership with you, with DHS and with our industry colleagues to enhance trust and make it as easy as possible for organizations to participate.

Thank you again for the opportunity to be here. I look forward to answering any of your questions.

[The prepared statement of Mr. Rosen follows:]

PREPARED STATEMENT OF MORDECAI ROSEN

JUNE 15, 2016

Chairman McCaul, Ranking Member Thompson and Members of the committee: Thank you for the opportunity to appear before you today. My name is Mordecai Rosen and I serve as senior vice president and general manager of the Security Business Unit at CA Technologies, where I manage global development of CA's cybersecurity products and solutions.

CA is one of the largest enterprise software companies in the world, serving global customers in nearly every major commercial and industrial sector. We are headquartered in New York, and have 11,000 employees across the globe, including many in districts represented on this committee. CA delivers software that is mission critical to the development, management, and security of technologies, which optimize business operations and enable digital transformation in what is being referred to as the "application economy."

I intend to focus my remarks today on two important and related topics. First, I want to highlight some of the emergent and serious cybersecurity threats we see in the application economy. Second, I'll plan to provide CA's specific perspective on the Cybersecurity Act of 2015—how it can be effectively implemented, and how we ultimately feel it can serve as a guidepost for reducing cyber risk in both Government and commercial systems.

INTRODUCTION

CA Technologies was a strong supporter of the Cybersecurity Act of 2015 and is encouraged by the implementation thus far. Cyber threat information sharing helps us improve our collective cyber defenses by enabling us to prioritize and deploy resources against current and anticipated attacks. Improving Federal agency cybersecurity helps defend National security and protect citizen data. We want to thank the committee for your driving this legislation over the finish line last year.

The application economy is transforming the way organizations do business. From entertainment to communications to finance, applications are rewriting the world in which we live, and are enabling organizations and governments to provide services to customers and citizens in new ways that reduce costs, enhance efficiencies, and improve outcomes. Software has become the principal means through which organizations deliver these new services. Examples of these technologies include mobile banking applications, the smart grid to reduce energy costs, and connected vehicle communications to improve safety and efficiency.

Applications have become the critical point of engagement for organizations of all sizes, optimizing experiences and providing a direct and constant connection from organizations to their end-users. CA software transforms businesses' ability to thrive in this new reality, delivering the means to deploy, monitor, and secure their technology investments.

However, the increasing volume and sophistication of cyber attacks threatens to undermine this progress through the illegal transfer of intellectual property, the theft of personally identifiable information (PII) and other sensitive data, and the undermining or destruction of critical infrastructure systems.

Cyber attacks that disable systems, such as the electric grid, water utilities, financial markets, or even mass transit systems, could have a potentially catastrophic effect, putting the health and safety of large populations at risk. Federal agency breaches that result in the loss of sensitive data can lead to massive identify theft and fraud, and can put National security at risk.

The Federal Government has suffered significant and harmful breaches over the past few years, most notably the Office of Personnel Management (OPM) breach that compromised the data of more than 20 million current and former Government employees and contractors. Yet, the Government doesn't stand alone as a target for attack. The critical infrastructure community of the United States includes public and private operators of critical systems and assets, and they are all experiencing sophisticated attacks that carry with them the possibility of catastrophic outcomes. The German government recently said in a report that hackers successfully broke into the control systems of a domestic steel plant and caused massive damage to the blast furnace. Here in the United States, the *Wall Street Journal* recently reported that 2 years ago hackers infiltrated the control system of a small dam less than 20 miles from New York City.

As the Federal Government and critical infrastructure owners and operators look to create efficiencies through automation and modernization, they must build security in to their systems on the front end and abandon the model of bolting security on afterwards.

THE ROLE OF IDENTITY PROTECTIONS IN ROBUST CYBERSECURITY

In this new threat environment, CA believes that identity and access management technologies are central to protecting systems, networks, devices, and data and to enabling secure interactions with customers and citizens. The traditional network perimeter can no longer provide a control mechanism for this access. Identities now constitute the new perimeter and are the single unifying control point across all apps, devices, data, and users. As such, identities and application programming interfaces (APIs) serve as the foundations of the application economy because they enable easier deployment of secure apps and help simplify control of access to those apps. They are how you protect access to apps and data, whether that be by human-to-machine or machine-to-machine. APIs provide a way to connect computer software components and data. Broadly speaking, APIs make it possible for organizations to open their backend data and functionality for reuse in new application services (think hotel websites using Google or Bing for their maps and directions).

An API achieves this by facilitating interactions between code modules, applications, and backend IT systems. The API specifies the way in which these different software components can interact with each other and enables content and data to be shared between components.

Given these new realities, identity is now the attack vector of choice for cyber criminals. In virtually every large network breach in recent memory, compromised identities were the common thread. Protecting identities is foundational to robust security in the application economy.

CA Technologies has made a strategic commitment to addressing identity-centric cybersecurity challenges in today's dynamic threat environment by developing effective identity management solutions through our in-house development process. CA software manages millions of user identities in most major countries around the world. We provide identity-centric security solutions to multiple Federal agencies. Our API Management tools are used within the Federal Government and the commercial sector to protect network and application interfaces, to facilitate the secure exchange of information, and to ensure that any data shared protects personal privacy. We believe all of these capabilities will further enable robust cyber threat information sharing. I'll touch more on this below.

DHS IMPLEMENTATION OF CYBER THREAT INFORMATION SHARING PROVISIONS IN THE CYBERSECURITY ACT

Congress passed the Cybersecurity Act of 2015 to help businesses and governments better protect themselves against cyber attacks. The Act promotes cybersecurity information sharing between the private sector and the Government, and across the private sector. In addition, the Act includes provisions to strengthen Federal agency cybersecurity through a Federal intrusion and detection system, through capabilities to continuously diagnose and mitigate cybersecurity risks, and through other measures.

CA Technologies supported the passage of the Cybersecurity Act of 2015 because it includes key provisions for which CA has been an active advocate: The bill includes targeted liability protections for program participants; it includes measures to protect the privacy of individuals; and it promotes the further development of automated mechanisms for sharing cyber threat indicators.

CA Technologies believes the Cybersecurity Act will enhance security and provide businesses with the assurances needed to securely share with trusted partners the security threats they are seeing on their own networks, and to receive threat indicators from the wider ecosystem, which will help them optimize defenses. We believe the automated capabilities provided through the DHS Automated Indicator Sharing (AIS) program will make it easier to accept and exchange cyber threat data in real time. CA Technologies welcomes the opportunity to provide our insight on implementation to date, and to make recommendations to encourage greater participation in the information sharing program and to improve Federal agency cybersecurity.

At the outset, I want to congratulate DHS for the job they've done thus far on implementation. The Cybersecurity Act of 2015 contained very aggressive time lines for DHS to release initial and final guidance to implement the program and to designate the primary system that would be used to exchange threat data between participants. DHS has met those deadlines thus far, and has worked collaboratively with their Government and industry partners to provide clarity around the overall requirements for sharing, the privacy protections and processes required to participate, and the process required to take full advantage of the program's benefits. We know how challenging it is to balance competing interests and meet very aggressive deadlines. While the initial guidance documents that DHS issued have raised some questions that we will address below, by and large we feel they provide good clarity on the technical, legal, and practical considerations entities need to weigh when determining whether to participate in the program.

We are encouraged by DHS's openness to the feedback they have received from industry, civil society, and other actors in the cybersecurity ecosystem, and by DHS's consultative approach. DHS has indicated that they intend to address the majority of these questions in their final guidance documents. We look forward to reviewing those in detail when they are released later today.

We are committed to working with DHS to move implementation forward with active and constructive industry dialogue. Among other organizations, CA Technologies is a member of the Information Technology Information Sharing and Analysis Center and sits on the Executive Committee of the IT Sector Coordinating Council, which helps advise DHS and other Federal agencies on information-sharing policies and public-private partnerships.

I'd now like to turn to our views on specific provisions of the legislation and the issues we see at play and where some further clarity is needed in implementation.

Liability Protection

Organizations should have targeted liability protection for the data they share or receive. This protection will encourage greater participation in the program, leading to better cyber defense. Liability and regulatory concerns are powerful inhibitors of participation in information sharing agreements. Reducing these barriers through targeted protections helps organizations feel more secure in sharing, receiving, and acting upon cyber threat indicators.

The Cybersecurity Act included targeted liability protections, and DHS today is releasing updated guidance providing greater clarification on these protections and the requisite responsibilities of participating companies.

Cybersecurity information sharing is based on trust, and this trust needs to be underpinned by strong certainty for participating companies. While the preliminary guidance released by DHS in February began to provide greater clarity around processes and procedures to gain protections, it also left a great deal of uncertainty. Our understanding is that the updated guidance should provide more clarity and we look forward to exploring this in greater depth. Beyond the release of the updated guidance, we encourage DHS to actively engage with industry and legal groups to help them better understand the information-sharing program, the responsibilities of participating organizations, and the liability protections that will be afforded participants.

Preserving Privacy

The Cybersecurity Act of 2015 requires organizations to take reasonable steps to remove PII of individuals not related to the threat from any cyber threat information they share through the program. It also requires the Government to further scrub this information to ensure that PII is removed. This is vital to protect the privacy of customers and citizens.

The global IT industry is very sensitive to issues of protecting customer privacy and enhancing trust in the solutions we deliver. Therefore, we believe it will be helpful for DHS and the administration to reassert that the purpose of cyber threat indicator information sharing is to protect networks.

Any Government exceptions to this purpose must be clearly defined and limited. In addition, CA and others advocated strongly that cybersecurity threat indicator information should be shared through a civilian portal under the legislation. We want to thank the committee for pushing the National Cybersecurity and Communications Integration Center (NCCIC) at DHS as the portal for information sharing, and we encourage the administration to continue to promote this portal as the principal mechanism through which to share.

While requirements to remove PII are important to protect privacy, it's also important to help organizations better understand how they can remove PII automatically. DHS's STIX/TAXII effort can help organizations understand what data to share, and how to share it, but companies will need further help to take the guesswork out of this process and automate the removal of PII before sharing. Myriad tools and capabilities exist in the commercial sector to enable automated PII removal. To the extent that organizations are able to effectively utilize these tools, it will lessen their concerns about liability and will heighten user confidence in the program.

We feel that the initial guidance released by DHS made strong commitments towards preserving privacy under this program, though participants will need greater clarity. We look forward to reviewing the updated DHS guidance in this space. Again, active stakeholder outreach and engagement throughout the policy implementation process can help lead to effective outcomes that address both security and privacy needs. DHS can work with sector-specific agencies to convene workshops and other engagement activities where organizations can learn best practices on privacy protection as part of information-sharing programs. Ideally, these workshops and programs can target different types of industries and can take place in different regions of the country.

DHS can also work to encourage greater participation in the information-sharing standards development process, established under the President's Executive Order from February 2015. The Standards Development Organization, led by the University of Texas at San Antonio in partnership with LMI, is currently developing draft standards for Information Sharing and Analysis Organizations (ISAOs). This work should be as open and inclusive as possible, enabling multiple types of organizations, including both nonprofit and for-profit organizations to establish ISAOs.

Automated Indicator Sharing

Ultimately, in order to truly move the needle on improving cyber defenses in a significant way, organizations will need to leverage automated, real-time, actionable information exchanges. Cyber attacks happen rapidly and without up-front notice. Once cyber threat indicators are discovered, this information must also be disseminated rapidly to allow organizations that are the subject of attacks to mitigate their impacts, and to help other organizations target their defenses against the newly-discovered threat.

DHS has been working to promote its Automated Information Sharing (AIS) program, which leverages explicit protocols to identify and structure information on cyber threat indicators and to provide for a secure manner of exchanging this information. CA Technologies has been working with DHS and other industry partners to help enable this secure, automated exchange of information across a wide range of different organizations.

CA provides API management software that helps authenticate, authorize, validate, transform, and filter near-real-time cyber-threat messaging. We believe that any successful information sharing program must depend heavily on the authentication of the individuals and organizations that participate, and on the validity and integrity of the information and the data that is shared under the program.

CA would like to thank the committee for promoting further development of automated information sharing mechanisms in the final legislation. While DHS's activity on automated sharing programs pre-dates the passage of the Cybersecurity Act, the inclusion of this program in the Act should boost confidence and encourage greater participation.

We recommend that DHS continue to leverage key outreach and partnership programs, such as the Critical Infrastructure Cyber Community or C3 program, and partnerships with Sector Coordinating Councils to build greater awareness around automated information sharing, and to help organizations understand what technical and procedural steps they will need to take to participate. Industry can also play a significant role to build awareness. Sector groups can develop user guidance and promote this with their members.

In addition, we recommend that DHS and the Federal Government continue to promote the STIX/TAXII protocols with global standards development organizations. Ultimately, cybersecurity is a global challenge that doesn't recognize National borders. Global security solutions providers, including CA Technologies, seek to develop products that can scale for the global marketplace. The STIX/TAXII protocols are already commonly used to enable cyber threat information sharing across the Federal Government and in the private sector, and we hope that this progress can be leveraged to improve cybersecurity internationally. DHS's recent decision to transition continued development of the STIX standard to OASIS is a positive development that will build international engagement and consensus around the protocol.

CA Technologies is not a current participant in the AIS system. Our internal security team currently utilizes multiple private-sector tools to identify, analyze, and prioritize cyber threat indicators. However, CA recognizes the significant benefits that we can derive from participation in information-sharing partnership programs in order to defend against cyber attacks. Therefore, we are actively exploring participation. We welcomed the passage of the Cybersecurity Act of 2015 because of its authorization of activities and its calls for protections for participants. However, while we have strong interest, we are being very deliberate in making a determination on participation because we have outstanding questions associated with the program.

First, will the information we receive through this program be timely, accessible, and actionable? Our security analysts must review and act on threat information from myriad sources in real time. Information shared through this program must help organizations to prevent, detect, or mitigate attacks. Therefore, information needs to be shared in an expedited fashion. Information has to be understandable for participants in the program. And participants need to be able to act on the information, whether that be mitigating against specific on-going threats, or re-deploying defenses for anticipated attacks. We continue to examine how we would need integrate AIS threat indicators into our overall threat management processes.

Second, how will DHS authenticate users who are receiving or sharing information in the program? Trust is vital to the success of information sharing and users must have confidence that the information they are sharing or receiving will not fall into the hands of adversaries and enable further attacks. Participants will want to know that the information they share will not be leveraged in a way that harms them. They will also want to know that the cyber threat indicator data they are acting on is valid. And, citizens and customers will want to know that participating businesses and the Government are doing everything they can to protect their privacy under this program. Therefore, identity and access management will play a crucial role in protecting the underlying information-sharing systems.

And third, will there be greater clarification and guidance around liability and privacy protections in the program? This includes clarification around liability protections for the sharing of information with other private-sector organizations and for acting or not acting upon the receipt of indicators. It also includes greater clarification on privacy protection requirements.

To reiterate, CA Technologies believes that DHS has done an admirable job of early-stage implementation of the information-sharing provisions of the Cybersecurity Act. CA looks forward to reviewing the updated guidance released by DHS today, which we hope will give us the certainty needed to become an active partner in AIS. We also encourage DHS to continue to conduct industry outreach, to help raise industry awareness of the programs, and to further provide clarification on associated liability and privacy protections.

We look forward to working with DHS and the committee on continued successful implementation of these programs.

PROTECTING FEDERAL INFORMATION SYSTEMS

A significant number of recent Federal breaches resulted from compromised identities, including those of privileged users. Title II of the Cybersecurity Act recognized this issue and authorized solutions to more fully address the vulnerabilities in Government systems.

The EINSTEIN and Continuous Diagnostics and Mitigation (CDM) programs, when fully deployed will help Government agencies acquire vital security capabilities and tools to better secure Government networks and systems.

The EINSTEIN program is designed to detect and block cyber attacks from compromising Federal agencies, and to use threat information detected in one agency to help other Government agencies and the private sector to protect themselves.

The CDM program provides Federal departments and agencies with capabilities and tools that identify cybersecurity risks on an on-going basis, prioritize these risks based upon potential impacts, and enable cybersecurity personnel to mitigate the most significant problems first. CA has been an active participant in the CDM implementation.

While CDM Phase 1 focused on asset discovery and management, Phase 2 is titled "Least Privilege and Infrastructure Integrity" and has prioritized both identity management and privileged access management. One of the most important areas of IT risk relates to privileged users. Whether inadvertent or malicious, improper actions by privileged users can have disastrous effects on IT operations and on the overall security and privacy of organizational assets and information. Therefore, it is essential that administrators be allowed to perform only those actions that are essential for their role-enabling "least privileged access" for reduced risk. Privileged Access Management solutions provide the visibility, monitoring, and control needed for those users and accounts that have the "keys to the kingdom." This visibility provides insight on activity and works to prevent or flag anything unusual that indicates security risk.

Both identity management and privileged access management positively affect operations, putting security activity in the background to make sure security is not seen as a barrier, but instead as an enabler to more secure business operations.

CA would like to thank the committee for authorizing these programs under the Cybersecurity Act. In particular, we believe that legislative language calling on the head of each agency to assess access controls to sensitive and mission critical data will help protect against the threat of improper use of privileged credentials.

Finally, on behalf of our IT industry partners, we would like to thank the committee for its help in conference negotiations to ensure that the EINSTEIN program would be designed to promote the security of Federal networks without jeopardizing multi-tenant cloud environments. In addition, we welcome continued committee oversight of DHS implementation to improve effectiveness and accountability.

Overall, our primary recommendations in this space are the need for procurement flexibility and improvements in the workforce development process. Currently, Federal agencies recognize the value in deploying CDM solutions. However, they recognize that these deployments could be paid for by DHS in the following appropriations cycle. Agility and speed are very important in this context. Ultimately, a plan and a strategy are worthless without deployment. There is a distinct risk of a moral hazard where agencies will not prioritize cyber funding in the short term, leaving them susceptible to risk of a significant breach in the interim.

Further, DHS partners with GSA on the development of contract vehicles for these programs, and there is a need for more trained contracting personnel to accelerate deployment of these new contract vehicles. We think this should be a key focus for implementation of Title III of the Cybersecurity Act.

In the wake of the OPM breach, we saw Government officials working around the clock to improve systems. These are committed individuals, and the sense of urgency following the breach resulted in quick and decisive action to resolve significant challenges that became immediately apparent. However, the long-term success in implementing those decisions may be hamstrung by backlogs in the procurement process.

Reacting to specific events to shore up defenses is different than proactive planning. As we look forward, we believe there is opportunity for DHS and its partner agencies to leverage the lessons learned in the cyber sprint and apply them proactively to enhance overall cyber posture across the Federal Government.

I would mention two things in particular that we think warrant further consideration by this committee. First, we believe it is critical for the Federal Government to align its own cybersecurity practices with the NIST Cybersecurity Framework that is quickly becoming the standard for private-sector information security management efforts. Ensuring that the same approach is being used across the public and private sectors will standardize terminology and ensure that the Government is walking the walk when it comes to the approach evangelized in the Cybersecurity framework. We want to commend the committee for favorably reporting the "Improving Small Business Cybersecurity Act of 2016" last week. As this legislation moves forward in the House and ultimately, we hope, to enactment, we would recommend that an explicit requirement be included directing DHS and the Small Business Development Centers to also leverage the NIST Framework in maturing their cybersecurity programs.

Second, we recommend the committee maintain focus on the unique cyber threats emanating from the compromise of digital identities. As we note above, the attack vector of choice in today's threat environment remains identity. CA believes that any conversations about cybersecurity threats and solutions must keep a strong focus on shoring up identity protections and enabling organizations to protect themselves from sophisticated identity-based attacks.

CONCLUSION

Cybersecurity represents a significant challenge for industry officials, and for State, National, and global policy makers. At the same time, the application economy is unlocking a multitude of opportunities to provide new services and value to customers and citizens. State, National, and global governments must work with private sector, academic, and public stakeholders to develop and implement cybersecurity policies that improve security, enable innovation, and build public trust.

The Cybersecurity Act of 2015 recognizes the crucial role of public-private partnerships in enhancing cybersecurity by authorizing and promoting active cyber threat indicator information sharing across the private and public sectors. It also recognizes the National imperative to protect Federal information networks and systems.

Ultimately, the success of this legislation will depend on stakeholder engagement, agility and inter-agency cooperation and buy-in. CA believes that DHS has made great strides in partnering effectively with the private sector on the implementation of information-sharing provisions and we encourage DHS to continue to improve in this regard. The Title II provisions of this Act, in combination with last year's updates to the Federal Information Security Management Act, further enhance DHS's position to play the lead operational role in protecting Federal information civilian systems.

CA Technologies applauds the efforts the committee has taken in tackling these key issues. We stand ready to continue partnering with the committee, DHS, and our industry colleagues in the effective implementation of the Cybersecurity Act of 2015.

Thank you very much for the opportunity to testify today, and I look forward to answering any questions you may have.

Mr. RATCLIFFE. Thank you, Mr. Rosen.

The Chair now recognizes Ms. Sage, for 5 minutes for her opening Statement.

STATEMENT OF OLA SAGE, FOUNDER AND CHIEF EXECUTIVE OFFICER, E-MANAGEMENT

Ms. SAGE. Good morning, Chairman Ratcliffe, Ranking Member Richmond, and distinguished Members of the committee. Thank you for the opportunity to testify this morning as a small-business owner of a 17-year-old tech firm on the Cybersecurity Information Sharing Act, CISA, and other information-sharing initiatives.

Today I will discuss my company's experience, some perspectives on CISA and some final thoughts.

In 2013, through our own research, we became aware of the DHS Enhanced Cybersecurity Services initiative, known as ECS, which is a voluntary information-sharing program that augments capabilities of critical infrastructure owners and operators by providing Classified cyber threat indicators to improve protection of their systems and customers.

Following the execution of a memorandum of agreement with DHS, we experienced a significant hurdle. We knew ECS was a Classified program, and while we had a facility clearance, it was not at the level required to gain access to information needed to determine if we could participate in ECS. We spent weeks trying to locate a SCIF, or a Sensitive Compartmented Information Facility, that we could use just for a few hours to review the requirements to be an ECS partner. We eventually found a solution, but to our disappointment the financial barrier to entry was so high we determined that it would be cost-prohibitive.

A year later, we entered into a Cooperative Research and Development Agreement, a CRADA, with DHS for an Unclassified program that allowed us to receive actionable Government-developed cybersecurity threat information and maintain access to or have an on-site presence within the National Cybersecurity and Communications Integration Center.

Our experience to date has been mixed. We do receive regular updates on threat information through the portal, which is very accessible. However, much of the Unclassified information is already widely available on the internet or is dated. We have ended up building our own TAXII server which provides communication specifications for exchanging cyber threat information through open sources.

In 2015, DHS informed us of another new program called the Automated Indicator Sharing dissemination capability. While we are interested in participating, establishing the necessary operational capabilities has been constrained by our own limited resources.

I would like to share 4 observations and a few thoughts on CISA and other information-sharing initiatives as it relates to small businesses like ours.

No. 1, small businesses are unaware of CISA. We recognize the law is new, and though it applies to any size organization, today it is largely an interest of larger companies with greater infrastructure and resources.

There is an opportunity for the Government to increase the visibility of the law through its existing outreach and awareness programs to the SMB community through, for example, SBA programs or by working with chambers of commerce, small-business associations and trade groups.

Second, small businesses need to understand how CISA helps them. In the law itself, there are only two references to small business, which highlights that this law is not directly focused on small businesses. How does CISA apply to SMBs in general? How does an SMB use CISA to help them better protect their business? What protocols would help facilitate and promote the sharing of cyber threat indicators within the SMB community?

Answers to these and other questions would help clarify the law's applicability SMBs.

Third, small businesses are confused by the myriad of information-sharing initiatives. The number and variety of information-sharing initiatives is overwhelming to many small businesses, if they are even aware they exist.

For example, Enhanced Cybersecurity Services, the Cooperative Research and Development Agreement, the National Cybersecurity Communications Integration Center, Automated Indicator Sharing, the Information Sharing and Analysis Centers and the Information Sharing and Analysis Organizations are just a few that we can participate in. It would be very helpful if these initiatives could be streamlined and tailored to our community.

Last, cybersecurity is costly for small businesses. Some industry estimates suggest costs of up to $60,000 a year for a 50-employee company, and it is not clear to many what the concrete benefits are of investing those kind of dollars in cybersecurity. As information-sharing is voluntary under CISA, the key driver for a small-business CEO like myself to consider participation is the cost to implement.

A significant percentage of small-business owners still do not believe that they have anything that criminals want. It would be helpful if there could be an estimate of what it would cost a small business to participate in various information-sharing forums, similar to the time estimates that are provided for completing Government forms.

In closing, CISA is in its early stages and we recognize that over time the implementation of the law will mature, providing more clarity for its application, in particular for small businesses. I remain committed to working with Government and industry partners to identify and promote affordable solutions that enable small businesses like ours to strengthen their cybersecurity readiness and posture.

Thank you again for the opportunity to testify and I am ready to answer any questions you may have.

[The prepared statement of Ms. Sage follows:]

PREPARED STATEMENT OF OLA SAGE

JUNE 15, 2016

OPENING REMARKS

Good morning Chairman Ratcliffe, Ranking Member Richmond, and distinguished Members of the committee. It is an honor for me to be here today.

My name is Ola Sage and I am the founder and CEO of two technology small businesses, e-Management and CyberRx, located in Silver Spring, Maryland. e-Management was founded in 1999 and employs nearly 70 information technology (IT) and cybersecurity professionals who deliver services in our core areas of IT Planning, Engineering, Application Development, and Cybersecurity. In 2013 e-Management was honored to receive the Department of Energy's Cybersecurity Innovative Technical Achievement Award, highlighting the capabilities of our cybersecurity experts in designing and implementing advanced cybersecurity detection and risk management capabilities. Earlier this year the U.S. Chamber of Commerce selected e-Management as one of the top 100 small businesses in America in 2016.

CyberRx, my second company, was launched in 2015 and offers a software platform that private-sector companies, and small businesses in particular, use to help them measure, manage, and improve their cybersecurity readiness. Our software allows companies to quickly assess their cyber readiness and resilience using a unique application of the Cybersecurity Framework (CSF), which was developed collaboratively with the National Institute of Standards and Technology (NIST), academia, and industry. CyberRx is both vendor-agnostic and affordable, as we believe cybersecurity should be manageable and accessible to all organizations, particularly the most vulnerable small- and medium-sized businesses (SMBs).

In April of this year, I was elected to serve as the chair of the IT Sector Coordinating Council (IT SCC). The IT SCC comprises the Nation's top IT companies, professional services firms, and trade associations, and works in partnership with the Department of Homeland Security (DHS) to address strategies for mitigating cybersecurity threats and risks to our Nation's critical infrastructure, especially for organizations and businesses that are particularly vulnerable, such as SMBs. One of the joint priorities this year with the IT SCC and DHS is to provide the SMB community with best practices and products for implementing the CSF to better protect businesses and manage risk.

I am also a 9-year member of Vistage, an international organization of more than 20,000 CEOs who control businesses that have annual sales ranging from $1 million to more than $1 billion. I regularly meet with and speak to small business CEOs in Vistage and other small business forums about why cybersecurity should matter to them and how it can affect their ability to keep business, stay in business, or get new business. Over the last 12 months alone, I have spoken to more than 200 SMB CEOs in a diverse mix of industries. I am a champion and advocate for SMB cybersecurity readiness.

Thank you for the opportunity to testify today as a small business owner.

In my testimony today, I will discuss:
- My company's experience with various Government information-sharing initiatives
- Perspectives on the Cybersecurity Information Sharing Act (CISA), and opportunities for the SMB community
- Concluding thoughts.

EXPERIENCE WITH GOVERNMENT INFORMATION-SHARING INITIATIVES

As an IT and cybersecurity small business provider, maintaining our competitiveness requires us to constantly add value to our clients by offering them the best combination of new products and services. In 2013, through our own research we became aware of the Enhanced Cybersecurity Services (ECS) program at DHS. ECS is a voluntary information-sharing program that augments capabilities of critical infrastructure owners and operators by providing Classified cyber threat "indicators" to improve protection of their systems and their customers. We reached out to learn more and were invited to establish a Memorandum of Agreement (MOA) to govern the Government's provision and e-Management's receipt and use of information and ECS-related activities.

Following the execution of the MOA, we experienced our first hurdle. We knew ECS was a Classified program and while we had a facility clearance, it was not at the level required to gain access to information needed to determine if we could participate in ECS. We spent weeks trying to locate a Sensitive Compartmented Information Facility (SCIF) that we could use just for a few hours to review the requirements to be an ECS partner. We reached out to various Government contractors whom we knew either had a SCIF or access to one, but were turned down time after time. We eventually found a solution that enabled us to review the requirements, but to our disappointment, the financial barrier to entry was so high, we determined that it would be cost-prohibitive for us to participate.

A year later, in 2014, we entered into a Cooperative Research and Development Agreement (CRADA) with DHS for an Unclassified program that allowed DHS and e-Management to engage in data flow and analytical collaboration activities, including receiving relevant, Unclassified, and actionable Government-developed cybersecurity threat information. Through the CRADA, e-Management was also permitted to maintain access to or have an on-site presence within the National Cybersecurity and Communications Integration Center (NCCIC).

Our experience with the CRADA has been mixed. We do receive regular updates on threat information through the portal, which is very accessible; However, much of the Unclassified information received is already widely available on the internet or is dated, and therefore has limited use for our cybersecurity analysts or our clients. We ended up building our own Trusted Automated eXchange of Indicator Information (TAXII) server, pulling from open sources to collect threat information that we could use to better protect our company.

In 2015, we were informed of a new initiative called the Automated Indicator Sharing Initiative Dissemination Capability, which could enable us to participate in the dissemination of cyber threat indicators under the DHS Automated Indicator Sharing (AIS) Initiative TAXII server, in addition to the existing portal means provided through our CRADA. While we have an an interest in participating, establishing the necessary operational capabilities is constrained by limited resources.

AN SMB CEO'S PERSPECTIVE ON OPPORTUNITIES FOR THE CISA AND INFORMATION-SHARING INITIATIVES FOR SMALL BUSINESSES

The Cybersecurity Act of 2015 provides a way for the Government and the private sector to collaborate on cybersecurity while providing the necessary protections to alleviate the concerns of many companies, large or small, that they may be exposed to civil or criminal liability, reputational damage, or competitive threats. Some observations about the law, other information sharing initiatives, and some recommendations for how CISA can be more relevant to the SMB community, are as follows.

1. Small businesses are unaware of CISA.—CISA is new and though it applies to any size organization, today it is largely an interest of larger companies that have the infrastructure and resources to act. There is an opportunity for the Government to increase the visibility of the law through its existing outreach and awareness programs to the SMB community through, for example, Small Business Administration (SBA) programs, or by working with Chambers of Commerce, small business associations, and trade groups.

2. Small businesses need to understand how CISA helps them.—In the law itself, there are only 2 references to small business, which highlights that this law is not directly focused on small businesses. How does CISA apply to SMBs in general? How does an SMB use CISA to help them better protect their business? Is CISA more applicable to certain types of small businesses? What protocols would help facilitate and promote the sharing of cyber threat indicators with the SBM community? Answers to these and other questions would help clarify the law's applicability to SMBs.

3. Small businesses are confused by the myriad of information-sharing initiatives.—The number and variety of information-sharing initiatives is overwhelming to many small businesses, if they are even aware they exist. For example, Enhanced Cybersecurity Services, the Cooperative Research and Development Agreement, the National Cybersecurity and Communications Integration Center, Automated Indicator Sharing, the Information Sharing and Analysis Centers, and/or the Information Sharing and Analysis Organizations, are just a few of the information-sharing initiatives companies can participate in. It would be helpful to the SMB community if these initiatives could be streamlined and tailored for the SMB community.

4. Cybersecurity is costly for small businesses.—Implementing cybersecurity best practices and solutions is costly for many small businesses. Some industry estimates suggest costs of up to $60,000 a year for a 50-employee company, and it is not clear to many what the concrete benefits are of investing those kinds of dollars in cybersecurity. As information sharing is voluntary under the law, the key driver for a small business CEO to consider participation will be the cost to implement. There is still a significant percentage of small businesses owners who do not believe that they have anything that criminals would want. It would be helpful if there could be an estimate, on average, of what it would cost a small business to participate in the information-sharing forum (e.g., similar to the time estimates that are provided for completing Government forms).

CONCLUSION

CISA is in its early stages and we recognize that over time the implementation of the law will mature providing more clarity for its application, particularly for SMBs. We at e-Management and CyberRx are committed to working with Government and industry to identify and promote affordable solutions that enable small businesses to strengthen their cybersecurity readiness and posture.

Thank you again for the opportunity to testify. I am ready to answer any questions you may have.

Mr. RATCLIFFE. Thank you, Ms. Sage.

Thanks to all the witness for your testimony.

I now recognize myself, for 5 minutes, for questions.

I will start by saying that after receiving today's hearing testimony, I want to try and make one thing clear, and that is that this subcommittee will try to do everything that we can to ensure that the final DHS and DOJ information-sharing guidance explicitly states and clarifies that the Cybersecurity Act's liability protections are in fact extended for sharing between non-Federal entities.

I would in fact like it noted for the record that it was Congress' full intent to grant private-to-private liability protections when such sharing was conducted in accordance with the law.

Having said that, I know that the Department of Homeland Security and Department of Justice this morning issued final guidance. I don't know if our witnesses have had an opportunity to review that, so I am not going to put any of you on the spot. But I would like to give you the opportunity to address this issue and how a lack of clarity in liability protection might cause general counsels in some private companies to prohibit their cyber operators from sharing information.

I will start with you, Mr. Eggers.

Mr. EGGERS. Thank you, Mr. Chairman.

I think, at least in terms of the interim guidance and procedures documents that we have been reviewing since February, our members view them as very good. I haven't had a chance to look through the latest documents that were just released, I think, over the evening. We'll do that. My impression, but we'll wait to see what the language states, is DHS and DOJ have tried to clarify, per the law, that the protections attach when non-Federal entities or private organizations or even State and local governments share between themselves and among themselves.

I think just kind of taking a step back, organizations are able to enter into the CISA and the AIS program when they are sharing threat data for a cybersecurity purpose, right, and they are doing other things, such as monitoring, sharing, receiving indicators and defensive measures.

Irrespective of the size of an organization, those protections and I should say the authorizations and the protections should attach.

Mr. RATCLIFFE. Thank you, Mr. Eggers.

Mr. Mayer, I want to give you an opportunity.

Mr. MAYER. Sure. Sure. Thank you.

Real quickly, I also haven't had an opportunity to read the guidance. I think this has its roots in perhaps some comments that came out of DHS at one point suggesting that there was some uncertainty or ambiguity around this issue. We had always felt that reading the statute that private-to-private sharing was permitted.

So I would say that, since some uncertainty was introduced, resolving that explicitly, as you did just now and as I am sure the guidance states, will only be helpful in terms of us being able to take advantage of the program. Thank you.

Mr. RATCLIFFE. Great. Thank you, Mr. Mayer.

Mr. Clancy, anything you would like to comment on?

Mr. CLANCY. Just to add, I think to, you know, build on the comments of the earlier panelists, I would just say that the place where the confusion was the greatest was in the ISAC community when sharing between a member to the ISAC to a member.

The ISACs themselves went and did their own legal reviews, got legal opinions and started to clarify that issue on their own. I think just reinforcing it by your statements and the additional clarified guidance from DHS and DOJ can help us move past this issue.

Mr. RATCLIFFE. Thank you, Mr. Clancy.

Mr. Rosen.

Mr. ROSEN. Yes, I think we primarily agree with what has been said down the line. We understand the existing liability we have today with sharing threat information, sharing breach information. We just want to make sure, and we will hopefully find it in the additional guidance, that we are not increasing our liability for either good-faith acts or lack of action based on some cybersecurity indicator.

So I think that kind-of is the most important clarity for us.

Mr. RATCLIFFE. Terrific. Thank you.

Ms. Sage, anything you would like to add?

Ms. SAGE. I haven't read it. Sorry, Mr. Chairman.

Mr. RATCLIFFE. No, that's fine.

Ms. SAGE. Happy to get back to you.

Mr. RATCLIFFE. On March 17, I was at the NCCIC to witness the certification to Congress that the Automated Information Sharing program, or AIS, was operational.

Mr. Clancy, you are the CEO of Soltra, which I understand is currently going through the process of connecting with DHS's AIS system, could you talk a little bit about how that process is going so far? What are the next big milestones for the AIS program going forward, as you see it?

Mr. CLANCY. Thanks for the question.

So yes, we have been enrolled in the program. We have been doing I will call it the technical integration side of the story. As with any new technical capability, there are those normal, you know, bumps in the road as you get going. We have been working through them and the Department's been pretty responsive in addressing them.

As I mentioned in my testimony, there are some challenges in the on-boarding, the process by which you get credentialed. To go to Mr. Rosen's comment, I think the challenge is establishing identity of the participants and the process that was used, vis-á-vis how it interacts with machine-to-machine sharing.

We believe that the other challenge was the customizations that were made and quite necessary for submitters of information to mark how they wanted their identity to be handled. So did they want comments attributed to them, to everyone in the program, to only U.S. Government or to no one outside of the NCCIC? That just takes time for the platforms and the implementers to absorb. So I think that's moving forward, I think it is in the right direction, but it had a little bit of latency for everyone getting started.

Mr. RATCLIFFE. Thank you, Mr. Clancy.

The Chair now recognizes the Ranking Minority Member of the subcommittee, the gentleman from Louisiana, Mr. Richmond, for any statement that he may offer or any questions he may have.

Mr. RICHMOND. Mr. Chairman. I would ask unanimous consent to submit for the record the DHS and Department of Justice document released this morning entitled Guidance to Assist Non-Federal Entities to Share Cyber Threat Indicators and Defensive Measures with Federal Entities Under the Cybersecurity Information Sharing Act.

Mr. RATCLIFFE. Without objection.*

Mr. RICHMOND. Thank you.

Let me start, I think, Ms. Sage, where you kind-of touched. The act requires periodic circulation of cybersecurity best practices, paying special attention to the needs of small businesses. When this guidance is published, presumably probably early next year, what would you like to see in it? I would take from your testimony that you mentioned, like, cost estimates and others, but anything else you would like specifically to see in it?

Ms. SAGE. Some degree of prioritization. Where should we start? Where are the areas that have the most impact to a small business like ours would also be helpful.

Mr. RICHMOND. Thank you.

Well, to Mr. Clancy, do you see potential conflicts between the FCC's proposed privacy rules for ISPs and the monitoring and information sharing authorized under the Cybersecurity Act?

Mr. CLANCY. I think that question might be better for Mr. Mayer, but I can certainly see any ambiguity in what the definition will add uncertainty and will chill the ability for people to share information.

Mr. RICHMOND. Mr. Mayer.

Mr. MAYER. Thank you, sir.

As I indicated in my opening remarks, I think that any time you introduce a level of uncertainty into this process, the lawyers are going to be inclined to want to be very prudent and careful.

What the FCC has done, well, let me correct that, what the FCC may do, because it is a proposed rulemaking, is they may have a standard in there that talks about being reasonably necessary versus the standard that is in the Act, which is that there has to be knowing that the information was not consistent with a cybersecurity purpose.

So what that means for us is that we understand what the bar is for knowing, we can understand what it is for gross negligence and willful misconduct. But when you are talking whenever it is reasonable, reasonably necessarily, we don't know if that means you should have known if you didn't know. We don't know where

---

the determination is going to be made after the fact as to what our instructions are, what the rules will require.

That is going to require probably another layer of legal scanning and review on the part of our attorneys. That really is very much inconsistent with what you are trying to accomplish with respect to real-time information sharing. So I am confident that we can work with the FCC and explain how that provision could complicate what was intended through this legislation.

Mr. RICHMOND. Thank you.

Well, in the lead-up to the Cybersecurity Act we passed, industry told us consistently over and over again that information sharing, the fear for participating was exposing oneself to legal liability.

In fact, Mr. Eggers, you specifically testified about a year ago to urge legislation granting businesses a safe harbor from frivolous lawsuits, public disclosure, regulatory and antitrust actions.

Ultimately, we passed that law. However, we talked with DHS this morning, and only about 30 entities are actually participating on a day-to-day basis. Some say a hundred have signed up, but only 30 have skin in the game. Would you say that the private sector is holding up its end of the bargain?

Mr. EGGERS. No, sir, I think that we've seen, as I noted in my opening testimony, we've kind of got two bookends. We've got companies that can't share enough and get enough cyber threat data. There are a lot of leading companies in this space that have been sharing and receiving data without protections for several years.

In that middle, I think, and the final guidelines just came out, so I think it is too soon to make a definitive judgment, but we are very optimistic.

On the other hand, we still have companies, as I noted I was at a DHS C3 event in Indianapolis, we still got companies who have, I think, pictures in their head of regulators lying in wait or consumer privacy groups writing lawsuits. That is the picture in their head. We don't think that that is completely accurate.

What we think is going to happen is the new protections, whether they are liability, regulatory, antitrust or public disclosure, are going to help those leading companies, right, and those folks who are part of ISAOs and ISACs now, or soon will be, do more confidently. Then I think over time and to the point about small businesses, I hope that what we will see is that we won't necessarily have to put a large burden on the smaller and under-resourced organizations.

There will be some kind of technologies, and I think they already exist, that can be put on networks and systems that can generate and swap threat indicators at real time. Those companies and that companies that help those organizations will enjoy those protections, too.

I also understand that there are about 30 companies that are directly plugged into the AIS system with about a hundred companies signed up. I expect that that number will grow as folks interpret the guidance and he ISAOs are created as we go forward.

Mr. RICHMOND. Thank you, Mr. Chairman. I yield back.

Mr. RATCLIFFE. Thank the Ranking Member.

The Chair now recognizes the gentlemen from Pennsylvania, Mr. Perry.

Mr. PERRY. Thank you, Mr. Chairman.

Ms. Sage, over here. In your opinion if you can, do you see the Federal Government's responsibility regarding vulnerability disclosure as a component of information-sharing process? Do you see the current level of vulnerability disclosures are strengthening your defensive posture, if that makes sense to you, if I have stated that correctly?

Ms. SAGE. If I understand the question, do I believe that the level of vulnerability information that we are receiving from the Federal Government is helping our companies?

Mr. PERRY. Essentially, correct.

Ms. SAGE. I would say probably, but there are just so many places to get it and it's overwhelming. We are not sure if we are getting the right information.

I welcome, you know, Matt Eggers' comment over there. If at some point this kind of information could be built into tools that we already use so that we are not having to go to all these different places to get it, that would be a very welcome development.

Mr. PERRY. OK. So somewhat of a consolidation and indexing if it so you know what is current and that you have the complete panoply of everything available at one place, you are not wondering if you are missing something.

Ms. SAGE. Correct.

Mr. PERRY. All right.

Ms. SAGE. To the comment of the AIS program, I mean, we were as I mentioned in my testimony, interested in participating, but in order to participate you have to have your own TAXII server.

Mr. PERRY. Right.

Ms. SAGE. So for a small business to invest in that, you know, it just adds to the cost.

Mr. PERRY. Right. Yes, I am not sure as to how you get there quite honestly.

Ms. SAGE. Right.

Mr. PERRY. But I appreciate the comment. Yes, I think it highlights an interesting aspect that maybe was not considered fully for sure.

Mr. EGGERS. Congressman Perry, if I may just offer up a thought?

Mr. PERRY. Sure.

Mr. EGGERS. I think what we are going to here is, I think we are going to have a situation where kind-of the vanguard of companies in ISACs and ISAOs are going to start moving out a lot more confidently and swiftly.

We've had really good discussions with policy makers and DHS, other Government bodies. I think we are really working together better than ever, at least in this space. But I do think that it is really tough for a small business who doesn't have paid professionals necessarily to do these kinds of things to expect them to have either the capital or the——

Mr. PERRY. Technical.

Mr. EGGERS [continuing]. The technical talent. So what we want to end up doing is we are going to innovate our way to where technology will help those small businesses keep doing what they are doing, whether they are inventing new drugs or what have you.

That technology will let them generate and receive threat data, and perhaps even kind-of heal, if you will, their networks and systems at real-time speeds. We are not there, but I think we will get there at some point.

Mr. PERRY. Yes, I appreciate that. As a former small-business owner myself, when I listen to this, I don't see how you get from point A to point B at the current position that we are. I think it is just exceptionally difficult.

Mr. ROSEN. Can I add one comment to the discussion?

Mr. PERRY. Sure.

Mr. ROSEN. So, we are a large business, $4 billion a year, 11,000 employees. Part of our analysis of AIS is the operational side.

So our organization is analyzing how it fits into our threat intelligence analytics engine, whether it is duplicate, whether it adds value, whether we can handle the feed, whether it adds . . . So that's us at $4 billion a year, 11,000 people, so I think that will give you some nature of what——

Mr. PERRY. Yes, so it is not just small business. I was going to ask you a question, Mr. Rosen, regarding the requisite tech refresh needed to ensure Federal networks. Do you think that they have the hardware or the software in network defense? I mean, do you get that sense now or do you think that they are lacking there?

Mr. ROSEN. I think they have made great progress since the cyber sprint last year, but it wasn't starting from a fantastic place to begin with.

Mr. PERRY. There is a new term right there, cyber sprint, I like that as well, at least new to me.

Mr. ROSEN. But the one thing I can suggest, is that in this Act and what DHS is doing, you have described the strategy and you have come up with the plan and you have come up with the metrics to measure it, but there is no security without deployment. That is where I think the focus has to wind up being.

We saw under emergency situations post-OPM breach, and CA was involved in the DHS cyber sprint where we were aggressively implementing PIV authentication and privilege access management throughout all the components, we operate very well when friction is reduced, and then you wind up having deployment and you have made genuine progress to securing the Nation. It's that gap, it's operationalizing the plan that I think has to wind up being the focus of whatever stumbling blocks there are in the way. You know, if they are acquisition-related, if they are technology-related.

I think the one thing you did a very good job of in the Act is not dictating technology. I think that was a really good thing. But I think that any focus that can help reduce the friction to deployment, how do we take that unbelievably effective sprint, and everybody pays attention to a sprint, the 100-yard dash, and how do we apply that to the marathon, which is our job, and divide it up in a way so people pay attention, friction is reduced and we can actually deploy? That's my recommendation.

Mr. PERRY. Thank you, Mr. Chairman. I yield.

Mr. RATCLIFFE. Thank the gentleman.

The Chair now recognizes the gentlelady from California, Ms. Sanchez.

Ms. SANCHEZ. Thank you, Mr. Chairman.

Well, as usual, we are at a spot where it's just all so over-whelming. I know so many of us on this committee have been working on this for such a long time.

I am worried about every aspect of business, large businesses, medium-sized businesses, technology companies, you know, we have only to look at the whole issue of Estonia a few years ago to understand that every business that uses IT can be hit. Whether it is just a threat of just taking your business off-line for a week while you are trying to figure it all out, or whether it's an imminent threat of taking all moneys out of everything, we are all concerned.

So I want to go back to the small-business issue because I think there is a lot of help with the larger companies. We deal with them all the time. We look at the banking industry, we have robustness et cetera.

Ms. Sage, I was very discouraged, quite frankly, after your frank and to-the-point testimony that you put forward. For a small business that is actually plugged in and aware in trying to work with the Department of Homeland Security programs, but can't leverage so many of those offerings unless you go through an established ISAC or a Sector Coordinating Council or any of the other layers that you mentioned in your testimony.

So a small-business owner who also happens to be the sitting chair of the IT–ISAC and to not meaningfully get access to how we are trying to help from the Department, I can't imagine what other smaller business are facing. I mean, they are throwing their hands up and saying I can't do this.

So is a small business best served by going through an ISAC? Is there a value proposition being offered from DHS to help small businesses? Can you from your interaction tell me what are the benefits of what we put in place under the cyber act and what are the biggest hurdles from your perspective for a small business?

Ms. SAGE. Thank you, Congresswoman. I didn't intend to make you depressed, so my apologies for that.

Ms. SANCHEZ. You know, I used to own a small business. So the biggest thing people need to understand about small-business owners is that they get some letter from the Government or something through the mail and fear strikes you, right? You didn't put somebody's tax moneys in the right way, you messed up on some IRA for your employees and there are penalties and the nasty letters. So, you know, in an effort to try to help people to actually secure their businesses and their information, it's really disappointing to have seen your testimony.

I love that you are frank, but what can we do?

Ms. SAGE. Well, you know, in our world it is all about simplification. Keep it simple.

So while it's great to have all of these choices, you know, cybersecurity, and I am speaking as a small business, you know, I have run my company for 17 years, we're about customers and growing our businesses, but we have so many different challenges that cybersecurity right now is just the latest one. Right? So whether, you know, we are worrying about payroll, we are worrying about employees as you know, and so we have now this huge thing, cybersecurity, that we are being told is going to wipe us out.

You know, Chairman Ratcliffe mentioned in his opening statements, there are two kinds of companies, the ones that have been hacked, the ones that don't know that they have. So there are lot of small businesses that I interact with who basically say if that is the case, why do I need to spend any more money? Because if we are already hacked and we just don't know it, why do I need to spend?

So I just think that, you know, I applaud what, you know, DHS and NIST, for example, did with the cybersecurity framework, the C3 program which I participated in some of their session and found the information very valuable. But I think, you know, and as you mentioned, I am one who is actually trying to get ahead of this. A lot of it is time. We just don't have the time to attend all of these different——

Ms. SANCHEZ. The resources, you don't have the personnel to put——

Ms. SAGE. Exactly. So I just go back to my point at the top, if there is a way to streamline, simplify, and prioritize these initiatives, I think that would be helpful.

Ms. SANCHEZ. Mr. Chairman, I didn't get to my second question, but maybe the panel can submit to this. Small businesses don't have the latest up-to-date software and the latest up-to-date hardware, and so is Department of Homeland Security working with programs of small businesses who have more dated equipment and technology? Or are we just moving to the forefront of what is the latest cutting edge? That would be my second question.

Mr. EGGERS. Congresswoman, if I may?

Let me maybe set a little bit, frame things. I think you are asking some very practical, good questions. Let me see if I can maybe frame things a little bit more——

Ms. SANCHEZ. Optimistic?

Mr. EGGERS [continuing]. Optimistically. So I think you are right. I think on a lot of levels you have got to cut small businesses some slack. I think that is the underlying kind of notion behind your concern. I think that is right.

On the other hand, I think small business obviously produce some of the most innovative products and services out there. So small doesn't necessarily mean not capable, but clearly our experience is, is that they are obviously the bulk of our membership.

We've got a campaign that we have been waiting for several years to get out to State and local chambers. We've hit 9 big cities in the last several years to promote the framework and really the solutions for all companies. Right? Then we also do, I mean, for example, we are going to be in San Antonio at the end of this month, we do smaller meetings with places like Beaumont, Texas, Longview, Texas. I will be in Green Bay in August. What we try to do is get out to our State and local chambers, just talk about some of the basic things that they need to do because they need help. Right? Some of the small businesses are actually ready to go and provide solutions.

I think one of the things that we can think about is trying to continue the education effort. Resources are an issue. I will note that there are a couple, if not more, businesses focused on small businesses in cyber, both here in the House and in the Senate, that will try to leverage entities like small business development centers. That looks like that could be pretty good.

The other thing I would note is in terms of, what do we tell businesses? I think we want to orient small business and companies and organizations of all sizes around the cybersecurity framework. If anything, I kind-of think of it as a written tool, maybe something companies can use to ask questions up and down from the CEO to the first hire. It is something that is really, I think, in a lot of ways, a mindset and it is also something that we want to focus on promoting here at home and globally.

Ms. SANCHEZ. Thank you, Mr. Chairman.

If the rest of the panel will submit that issue of, you know, what are your ideas for small business? I would really appreciate it.

Thank you for the indulgence.

Mr. RATCLIFFE. I thank the gentlelady.

For the record and for the benefit of some in the audience and for a point of optimism on this question and issue, last week this committee did mark up and pass legislation to support small businesses. H.R. 5064 is the Improving Small Business Cybersecurity Act, and the bill, if it became law, would require DHS to work with the Small Business Administration to jointly develop a strategy to aid small businesses. So hopefully that will, to address some of the issues that have been raised here, move forward for consideration by the full House.

With that, I will recognize the gentleman from Rhode Island, Mr. Langevin.

Mr. LANGEVIN. Thank you, Mr. Chairman.

I want to thank our panel for our testimony today and Mr. Chairman, especially I want to thank you and the Ranking Member for holding this hearing.

As you know many of us, Chairman McCaul and I and many others, have been trying for years to get information-sharing legislation passed. Thankfully, the leadership of this Congress and last year, we finally passed that legislation. Now comes the implementation and holding hearings like this and making sure that we are implementing it the right ways is vitally important.

Before I begin my questions, I just wanted to mention, Mr. Eggers, I want to thank you for mentioning the work that Chairman McCaul and I have been doing on the Wassenaar Arrangement. I think we are moving in a good direction on that.

I also want to say, you know, how much I appreciate the chamber being so proactive on Wassenaar. It has been very helpful in getting it to a good place.

But to my questions, if I could, following up on Mr. Richmond's question, I think you all touched on this issue in your written testimony, but as directly as possible, again why is the uptake of AIS so low given Mr. Clancy's testimony that one can be up and running with a Soltra install in as few as 15 minutes? So, you know, I find it hard to understand why more mature companies wouldn't at least be experimenting with the threat stream.

Again, I understand the guidance for sharing with DHS is just being finalized, but why wouldn't they at least be receiving data from the Government when there is known threat indicators and applying those to their cyber defenses?

Mr. EGGERS. Is that for me, sir?

Mr. LANGEVIN. For the panel.

Mr. EGGERS. I will jump in. Thanks for your comments about Wassenaar.

I would say discussions are progressing on that front. We have been encouraging our colleagues in Europe to engage European and Wassenaar officials that handle cyber and export-control issues. I think we have made progress thanks to you all here, but we are not out of the woods yet.

A nod to the administration for saying that the cyber controls in that space need considerable work, if not, our preference, elimination.

Now, in terms of sign-up, you know, I might say, gosh, the AIS system was turned on, if you will, formally in March. The final guidance just came out. We are pretty optimistic that things will keep moving.

In my mind, what I think we're trying to do is to make sure that we're moving and grooving with our largest and most sophisticated organizations that can tap in, if they are not already tapped in, tomorrow and then make sure that we are boosting the confidence of companies that are on the sidelines waiting to see how policymakers handle this issue. I think the key word is trust.

I think, as I noted in my opening remarks, we've got a, let's say, a representative company that says, hey, we have heard about CISA, but it is not exactly clear yet if this program will work for us or against us. I think they have got still, I would say, somewhat legitimate fears about liability, but I think the program is such that that should minimize those fears.

The other thing is, is we want to make sure that regulators are kept at bay in terms of the data that they receive. But I think on balance, we would say jump in, get involved as appropriate.

Mr. LANGEVIN. Yes, and just on that, I understand that on the business side of building the trust on sharing the information with the Government. That I get, even though it is voluntary, but I am talking about actually receiving from the information, from the Government, not what private sector would share with Government, yet. I understand that trust will be come in time and hopefully soon. But at least accepting information from the Government where there are known threat indicators, why not at least accept it?

Mr. EGGERS. Yes, I think most companies are probably more than happy to receive, rather than share. Right? Because when you share, then you are putting yourself out there and your data out there. But I will finish there and see if others here on the panel have thoughts.

Mr. CLANCY. So a few thoughts for you. I think there is a technical dimension and operational dimension. On the technical dimension, platforms like mine need to complete our certification that we can fully support bidirectional communication with AIS. Because of those adjustments that were made, we had to make some code changes and we are going through that process.

I think one of the barriers and I mentioned it in my testimony is there is no actual test system to use with DHS. So in their rush to produce the platform and make it live, they didn't have, you know, an extra system, if you would, where you can go test things out, and so you want to be very sure before you turn things on in production. I think that's one piece.

On the operational side, I think there are just some mechanical issues that need to get worked through with signing up. I mentioned earlier the credentialing process. That process that is being leveraged was really set up to get individuals encryption certificates so they can send secure email or authenticate as individual humans to websites. That provisioning process wasn't designed for machine-to-machine sharing. A simple example is, all of the issuance processes assumes you are using Windows desktop. Our service platform is a Linux workstation, it is a completely different technical environment. So we have to add wizards and helpers to help people import those credentials to get them to work. So there are those kind of pieces.

Then there is a tiny bit of thing on the agreement side where you sign one agreement, you get some paperwork back, you have to sign a second agreement and put it through. If I can take that to my general counsel once, it will take weeks out of the process because I need to get back in their queue to review agreement No. 2. So it is little things like that I think will help.

We are early. I mean, the law is 6 months old. The program is only 3 months old. So I think it is just, you know, if we have this problem again in 12 months then we are in a very different place.

Mr. MAYER. I would like to offer some comments on that. Building on what's been said previously, I think the fact that we have 30 companies that are operational right now, frankly, given the scope of engagement that is required at the financial level, at the operational level, at the technical level, at the legal review level, is not a bad situation. In fact, Mr. Clancy talks about not having the test bed environment. The live environment has, in a sense, become part of the test bed process right now. So for example, I can speak to a company in our sector where they did try to work through the AIS engagement. I think Mr. Clancy can substantiate this, and DHS has acknowledged this, that there is legacy data in the systems that has triggered some reaction that was not anticipated. It's delaying the process of AIS. That is something that can be overcome. They are talking about 6.2.0. We have guidance that is still coming out as recently as this morning.

So I think that the prudent thing for a lot of companies right now is to see these issues get resolved, to understand what the value proposition is for them, to work with DHS and other sectors to see what we can do to expedite and facilitate a more streamlined process. I think that will happen, but expecting that all to be resolved in 6 months is probably a little bit, I don't know what the word is, overly optimistic or whatever. But progress is being made.

Mr. LANGEVIN. Thank you. I know my time is expired, so I don't know if—OK.

Mr. EGGERS. Mr. Ratcliffe——

Mr. ROSEN. I thought I would just give a brief response from our perspective. So I think other than the issues that we have discussed on clarification of liability and even what do we mean by PII data and privacy, and especially for a global company where, you know, we have, you know, general data protection regulation coming out of the European Union, so we have to look at it from a lot of aspects. But other than that, we are looking at it very similar to what just got described from an operational point of view and a priority point of view.

So we have a broad threat intelligence feed and analytics engine inside of our company to protect it, to protect our company. We are in the process of exploring what this looks like, how do we add that to the feed, does it generate additional work for our operations, how do we tune it? So that will be our next step in exploring it once the clarifications on the privacy and liability issues get put by the wayside. Again, bringing it to general counsel once is better than bringing it multiple times.

I do think this idea of having a test bed for folks like us to try it, get the data feed, do the analytics, see what the impact is, it is really an operational and priority issue for us. But we believe, if the data feeds aren't what we are getting today, meaning if it is not duplicative data, you know, the more intel feeds for us, the better.

Mr. LANGEVIN. Sure. Very good. Thank you. I will mention, too, that one of the things that I am not clear on yet, too, is that the ISACs have not signed up for this yet either, so it is not just a problem with businesses not yet signing up, it is also the ISACs, which are designed for information sharing, have not yet signed up. I find that troubling and hopefully we will move it to a better place in the very near future. So, thank you, Mr. Chairman. I yield back.

Mr. RATCLIFFE. Thank the gentleman.

The Chair now recognizes my colleague from the great State of Texas, Ms. Jackson Lee.

Ms. JACKSON LEE. I thank the Chairman very much.

Chairman Ratcliffe, let me thank you and Ranking Member Richmond for being so diligent on these issues.

I am going to stay narrowly focused and say somewhat of the obvious. I am glad that we passed the Oversight of the Cybersecurity Act of 2015 and included privacy elements in that bill as well, and now that we are having an oversight of the Oversight bill to find ways to improve our service to the American people.

But I want to be the one that poses or at least puts in the record that we are dealing with fire here. We are dealing with something that probably is not evidenced in the calmness of our conversation. But I hope you will view this committee as being very serious about this issue.

So I am going to ask to put into the record, Mr. Chairman, the "Crime Pays: Ransomware Bosses Make $90K Annually." It speaks to the Russian ransomware boss making $90,000 a year, or 13 times the average income for citizens in the country who stick to the straight and narrow. Of course, their job is to maintain, update it so that the antivirus systems won't recognize the software that they are maintaining as malware. So I ask unanimous consent to place that into the record.

Mr. RATCLIFFE. Without objection.

[The information follows:]

ARTICLE SUBMITTED FOR THE RECORD BY HONORABLE SHEILA JACKSON LEE

SPOTLIGHT ON SECURITY.—CRIME PAYS: RANSOMWARE BOSSES MAKE $90K ANNUALLY

By John P. Mello Jr., June 14, 2016, 5 o'clock AM PT

http://www.technewsworld.com/story/83603.html

If crime doesn't pay, Russian ransomware bosses wouldn't know it.

The average Russian ransomware boss makes US$90,000 a year—or 13 times the average income for citizens in the country who stick to the "straight and narrow," according to a recent Flashpoint study.

What does a ransomware honcho do for those rubles? Basically, the job calls for supporting and maintaining the malware.

"The software has to be constantly updated so that antivirus systems won't recognize it as malware," explained Vitali Kremez, a cybercrime intelligence analyst with Flashpoint.

"It's not a situation where you provide the malware and sit back on a couch waiting for your payments. You have to work on it on a daily basis," he told TechNewsWorld. "The boss controls the source code for the malware."

RANSOMWARE AS A SERVICE

The malware model is evolving, according to the Flashpoint study, which focuses on the Russian ransomware scene.

"A new form of ransomware has been developed that is in effect 'Ransomware as a Service' (RaaS)," notes the report. It "enables 'affiliates' to obtain a piece of ransomware from a crime boss and distribute it to victims as these affiliates wish."

That's a departure from the past, when ransomware was available only to criminals willing to make a hefty upfront payment for the malware—$2,000 to rent or $5,000 to buy. That began to change last November, Kremez noted.

"We started to see developers considering giving their malware free of charge to criminals and keeping 40 to 50 percent of each ransomware payment made," he said.

The new business model has lowered the barriers to getting into the business. It is not particularly hard for newcomers to start spreading ransomware quickly. They can attack corporations and individuals through botnet installs, email and social media phishing campaigns, compromised dedicated servers and file-sharing websites.

"It used to be a one-on-one business," Kremez said. "At this stage, it's all automated. We see marketplaces. We see services on the dark web where you deposit your money and buy what you have to buy without any direct communication with the seller."

MALICIOUS INFRASTRUCTURE GROWING

More evidence of the popularity of ransomware is evident in Infoblox's latest quarterly report on malicious infrastructure building globally.

To measure that kind of activity worldwide, Infoblox has created a threat index. Upon its launch in the first quarter of 2013, the threat index was 76. During this year's first quarter, the index reached it's highest point ever: 137.

Activity related to ransomware has fueled the index's rise.

"While exploit kits remain a major threat, this latest jump was driven in large part by a 35X increase in creation of domains for ransomware over the previous quarter, which in turn drove an increase of 290 percent in the overall malware category," the report States.

The activity of malware kit developers is another indicator of ransomware's attractiveness to criminals. Kits are used to infect devices with a variety of malware programs.

"A number of exploit kits and threat actor gangs behind them have started adding ransomware to their repertoire over the last few months," said Sean Tierney, director of cyber intelligence at Infoblox.

"These are gangs that were using their kits to deliver other kinds of malware," he told TechNewsWorld, that "have either started including or switched entirely to ransomware."

It's likely that the ransomware market will level off as security software makers get better at detecting it and consumers get smarter about avoiding it, suggested Tierney.

"Then the market will become saturated," he said, "and the return won't be able to support the amount of activity going on."

EXPANDING 2FA

Two-factor authentication, which requires both something you have and something you know in order to access an account, has proven to be a good way to thwart data thieves. One problem with the technology, though, is that it isn't easy for many rank-and-file developers to deploy. One authentication company aims to change that with a recently launched program.

Centrify actually goes beyond 2FA to include single sign-in—which allows the use of a single set of credentials to log into multiple accounts—along with password reset and access control of a device. Under the program, developers can plug into those features through Centrify system APIs.

"Developers who are building an application from a great idea aren't necessarily expert in security," said Chris Webber. security strategist at Centrify.

"We can give that to them," he told TechNewsWorld.

"They can take advantage of all the user management and multifactor authentication that Centrify's built, so they don't have to learn about that world and can concentrate on their great idea," Webber pointed out. "It's more and more critical that we need to figure out how to put two-factor auth everywhere, because passwords alone are just not a great way to do authentication anymore."

BREACH DIARY

- May 30. Troy Hunt, who maintains the data breach awareness portal Have I Been Pwned, advises his subscribers that information on 65 million Tumblr accounts is being offered for sale on the dark web.
- May 30. Twitter account of Katy Perry breached and her 89 million followers sent tweets filled with profanity and slurs, TechCrunch reports.
- May 31. MySpace announces it has reset the passwords of all accounts created prior to June 11, 2014, due to a data breach.
- May 31. A Federal district court in Pheonix, Arizona, rules that insurance provider Chubb does not have to reimburse P.F. Chang under a cybersecurity policy for payments to credit card processors connected to a 2014 data breach.
- June 1. U.S. Federal Reserve detected more than 50 breaches between 2011 and 2015, including several incidents described in internal documents as espionage, Reuters reports.
- June 1. Medical information of thousands of NFL players is at risk after backback containing the data was stolen from an athletic trainer's car, Deadspin reports.
- June 1. FBI alerts public that extortion attempts are being made against victims whose personal information has been compromised in recent large data breaches. Extortionists are threatening to make victim's personal informtion public if not paid two to five bitcoins.
- June 1. TeamViewer reports it experienced a service outage due to a DDoS attack, but its systems were not breached by hackers.
- June 2. Medical records of some 40,491 customers of the Stamford Podiatry Group in Connecticut impacted due to a system intrusion, HealthIT Security reports.
- June 2. 2015 payroll tax data of employees of Verify Health Systems in California at risk after an employee was duped by a phishing scam, SC Magazine reports.

Ms. JACKSON LEE. Speak the obvious of the hacking of the Democratic National Committee, which brings it really home. For those of us young enough to remember Watergate, we are managing now 21st Century. But again, the individuals allegedly attached to that were Russian. I don't speak particularly to Russia, but it does say that this is an international threat that goes to our private sector.

Some years back I chaired the Transportation Security Subcommittee, and this component was under that committee. I remember noting the 80 percent-plus cyber issues would be in the private sector. So I am glad of your presence here today.

Then I want to ask unanimous consent to put into the record "Lights Out: A Cyberattack, A Nation Unprepared, Surviving the Aftermath." That is, of course, a bestseller investigation by Ted Koppel.

Mr. RATCLIFFE. Without objection.*

Ms. JACKSON LEE. So I want to go first to Ms. Sage and indicate, if I could, very briefly for your answer. Pointedly, you indicated that the information was dated. And that you, I guess, on your receiving end needed a secure entity. Help me understand what we can do to help. Obviously, I want the data to be current. I don't want it to be where you have just turned on National news and said, well, I just saw this on the National news. Then, is the idea of a secure channel yours or ours? Or how can we help you do that?

Ms. SAGE. Sure. Thank you, Congresswoman, for your question. The Enhanced Cybersecurity Services initiative is the one that is a Classified program. That was the one where we had difficulty getting access to a facility where we could even just review the requirements, not even whether or not we were going to participate. So there, if there is a way for DHS or the Government or some Government entity to be able to provide those kinds of facilities so that companies—and we had a clearance, it just wasn't at the level, you know, needed to be able to review these requirements—to make that easier, that would be very helpful. Because we actually had to start looking at, did we need to build a SCIF, and those costs are just cost-prohibitive.

Then, you know, without even getting into the merits of the program itself, once we were able to review, it just was not something that a small business would be—and there are two pieces to that program. You can be a provider or you can partner with the larger firms. So that's now kind-of what we are exploring, because, you know, trying to invest, is just not possible.

On the question of data, and this also speaks, I think, to the AIS initiative, I think at the end of the day, I agree with what, you know, my colleagues have talked about in terms of financial, technical, and operational considerations. But I think it all, at the end of the day, comes down to the quality and the value of the data that is received.

So it was our experience with the CRADA, when we participated in the Unclassified program, that a lot of the data that we were receiving through the portal was already widely available. So it was just another stream of data that was not particularly adding, you know, value above and beyond.

So I can't speak, you know, and I believe the AIS program is a good initiative, and I would just urge on the DHS side and the Government side that as that data is being provided, that it is reviewed for the quality and the currency to the recipients.

Ms. JACKSON LEE. I think, Mr. Chairman, this is something that we really pointedly can look at together with DHS on the accuracy or the currency of the data.

Mr. Chairman, I have just one or two points and I will be finished. I thank you.

One is going to be deviating, because I made a commitment that I would make mention of this, whatever Homeland Security meeting I was in, and that is, of course, to acknowledge my sympathy for those who lost their lives this past Sunday, the most heinous

---

*The information has been retained in committee files.

and largest mass murder, massacre, and slaughter of American people here in the United States in our history.

I believe that there is a great deal of morality in this Congress, and so I am hoping and looking for action this week on a ban on the assault weapons.

No. 2, no-fly, no-buy. If you are on a terrorist watch list, you should not be able to buy assault weapons. Something to say to the American people that we get it, that our pain is as deeply embedded as theirs, that families who mourn tragically do not mourn in vain. I am hoping that this Homeland Security Committee can be a bipartisan leader on these issues.

I hope the American people and those who are listening in this audience in their own way will rise up and be actively engaged in ensuring that we are responsive to the deeply embedded pain. I asked the question whether or not we are in fact good Samaritans and whether or not it is your neighbor, and if it is your neighbor, what would you do? If it is yourself, what would you do?

So I am looking forward to us working on that issue.

But let me conclude my remarks on the cybersecurity and raise this question out of Ted Koppel's article. Maybe some of you have read his book.

So, Mr. Eggers, I am going to go to you because you represent a vast number of private sector. So I won't read it all, but Mr. Koppel suggests that a massive cyber attack, we would have no running water, no refrigeration or light, food and medical supplies dwindling, we would be going in the dark, banks no longer function, looting is widespread, law and order are being tested as never before.

What is your response to the private sector's preparation for what might be? Because we have to answer those questions.

Mr. EGGERS. Congresswoman, good to see you.

Ms. JACKSON LEE. Thank you.

Mr. EGGERS. You know, I think in a lot of ways, and hearing Mr. Koppel speak, I get the sense more he uses kind-of the electric sector as kind-of a gateway for his concerns. I think it's less about that, it's more about some kind of dystopian future, right? But I think what he leaves out, if you talk to folks in the administration and the private sector, they are going to say, you know what, the book paints the private sector and Government as if we are sitting still, when in fact there is so much going on, not only in the electric sector and other sectors that frankly even individuals like myself, I can't keep up.

So leaving aside the regulatory platform that the electric sector works under, I am pleased to hear situations where, let's see, I think Secretary Spalding recently said, hey, look at what has happened in Ukraine with an incident with their electric sector. We know how to handle that here.

Now, I am the last person that is going to say an incident won't impact us, but when I think about the Sector Coordinating Councils, the ISACs and ISAOs, our organization of critical infrastructure at greatest risk, we know who those folks are. I would say, if anything, we are pretty busy. One of the things that I think we need to focus on is making sure that they have got everything they need for a bad day.

The other thing is we often point the fingers at ourselves, right? I like this program, CISA and AIS, because we are working together pretty well. The chamber just approved a norms and deterrence statement last week, our board of directors, saying at least a couple of things. We impose a lot of costs on ourselves, but we can do better in an active, restrained, legal way to impose costs on bad guys. We are doing that.

But let me give you an example. So the Cyber Forum of Independent and Executive Branch Regulators, there is something like a dozen or so agencies in that body. If I look at organizations like the Secret Service or DHS that are positioned to push back, that's two. I am not saying we act recklessly, but I am saying that we need to be mindful about how we impose costs on bad actors, many of whom or which are State actors or their proxies or super criminal groups.

So when I think about small business or even larger companies, I think that they are going to be ultimately resource-constrained against a nation-state or their surrogates. I hope that helps.

Ms. JACKSON LEE. It does.

I will just end, Mr. Chairman and say, as I heard some good news from Mr. Eggers, I want to emphasize that I think we need a SOS or Red Cross team dealing with cybersecurity in light of these possibilities. I yield back. Thank you.

Mr. RATCLIFFE. Thank the gentlelady.

I wish we could do another round of questions, but prior commitments of the Chair prevent that. So I will thank the witnesses for your valuable and important testimony today, and I thank all the Members for their questions.

Members of this committee, I think, will have some additional questions for the witnesses. That being the case, we will ask you to respond to those in writing.

Pursuant to committee rule 7(e), the hearing record will be held open for a period of 10 days.

Without objection, the subcommittee stands adjourned.

[Whereupon, at 11:41 a.m., the subcommittee was adjourned.]

APPENDIX

QUESTIONS FROM CHAIRMAN JOHN L. RATCLIFFE FOR MATTHEW J. EGGERS

Question 1. Does the U.S. Chamber of Commerce believe that the Cybersecurity Act of 2015, specifically Automated Indicator Sharing, is applicable to all businesses, including small businesses, and private organizations?

Answer. The chamber believes that the Cybersecurity Act of 2015—particularly title I, the Cybersecurity Information Sharing Act of 2015 (CISA)—and Automated Indicator Sharing (AIS) are applicable to businesses and private organizations of all sizes and sectors.

Question 2. What avenues do Government and industry have to increase businesses' awareness of the Cybersecurity Act of 2015, specifically Automated Indicator Sharing?

Do you expect that all businesses, especially small ones, will use the Cybersecurity Act of 2015, specifically the Automated Indicator Sharing program, directly?

Answer. There are many ways to publicly promote CISA. The chamber led the Protecting America's Cyber Networks Coalition, a partnership of more than 50 leading business associations representing nearly every sector of the U.S. economy to pass CISA. Each association has on average thousands of members.

The chamber is championing CISA as part of our cybersecurity campaign, which was launched in 2014. This National initiative recommends that businesses of all sizes and sectors adopt fundamental internet security practices, including the joint industry-National Institute of Standards and Technology (NIST) Framework for Improving Critical Infrastructure Cybersecurity (the framework) and the new information-sharing law.

The chamber spearheaded 11 major regional roundtables and 2 summits in Washington, DC. More events are planned for 2017. The chamber's Fifth Annual Cybersecurity Summit was held on September 27. Each regional event had approximately 200 attendees and typically features cybersecurity principals from the White House, Department of Homeland Security (DHS), NIST, and local FBI and Secret Service officials.

The chamber also partners with State and local chambers and universities to produce cyber educational events in locations such as Appleton, Wisconsin; Augusta, Georgia; Oak Brook, Illinois; Indianapolis, Indiana; Irving, Texas; and Longview, Texas. We endorse CISA and AIS at each gathering. In addition, chamber professionals regularly speak on and/or moderate industry panels tied to cybersecurity, where we can actively pitch CISA/AIS to multiple businesses.

DHS Deputy Secretary Ali Mayorkas addressed the chamber's Small Business Summit on June 14, and he advocated that businesses take basic, prudent steps to protect their devices and sensitive data, including leveraging cybersecurity information-sharing services.

Big picture: The chamber is urging businesses to use the framework, join an information-sharing body, and take advantage of the CISA/AIS system as appropriate. We are pressing senior leaders of industry groups to popularize these initiatives among their peers and constituencies, including through jointly written chamber-DHS op-ed articles.[1]

The chamber commends DHS and the Department of Justice (DOJ) for jointly holding their Cybersecurity Conference for Lawyers on September 28, which included a discussion on traditional challenges to sharing threat data and CISA's attempt to address these challenges and a demonstration of the AIS program.

Question 3. The issue of how many entities are signed up for the Automated Indicator Sharing program was discussed at the hearing. Should Information Sharing

---

[1] *http://thehill.com/blogs/congress-blog/technology/304163-cybersecurity-building-resiliency-together, www.csoonline.com/article/3124626/security/advancing-cybersecurity-through-automated-indicator-sharing.html.*

and Analysis Organizations (ISAO)—and Information Sharing and Analysis Centers (ISAC)—participating entities be included in the accounting of the number of participating entities under the program if they are sharing cyber threat data through an ISAO or ISAC that is plugged into DHS's NCCIC?

Answer. First, it is important to stress the chamber believes that the success of CISA and AIS should not be linked to the number of organizations that sign up for AIS. Some subcommittee Members suggested at the hearing that the number of AIS signers and the achievements of CISA/AIS are bound together. Most industry organizations are unlikely to share cyber threat indicators (CTIs) directly with Government partners. Instead, the chamber believes that the vast majority of businesses will share and receive cyber threat data with industry peers and ISACs and ISAOs. It is our understanding that most businesses will use information-sharing bodies as conduits between themselves and DHS, among other Federal entities. These businesses will not be signed up with AIS, but significant amounts of information sharing will nonetheless take place.

Second, ISAOs and ISACs and their respective members should be part of the calculation of private organizations that are possibly using CISA/AIS. The chamber defers to DHS's data concerning AIS involvement. Yet at the time of this writing, we understand that approximately 150 private organizations have signed DHS's Terms of Use that govern the use of CTIs and DMs and participation in the AIS initiative.[2] Fifty-eight of these organizations are attached to the AIS server and consume Government-furnished CTIs. In addition, 12 of these organizations are either ISACs or ISAOs. For instance, the Financial Services–ISAC (FS–ISAC) has upward of 7,000 member financial institutions and partner organizations. Presumably, many of these entities are engaged in protected information sharing under CISA but may not be part of AIS accounting.[3]

Similarly, the Health Information Trust Alliance (HITRUST) Cyber Threat XChange, the health industry's ISAO, is now connected to AIS and supports the bidirectional sharing of cyber threat data with DHS. The real-time sharing of CTIs between HITRUST's more than 1,000 members and DHS helps private-sector organizations reduce their cyber risks.[4]

The chamber understands that several entities are testing the sharing process before they initiate automated, bidirectional sharing on routine basis.

QUESTIONS FROM RANKING MEMBER CEDRIC L. RICHMOND FOR MATTHEW J. EGGERS

Question 1a. In accordance with §1A103 and § 105(a)(4) of the Cybersecurity Act of 2015 (Pub. L. No. 114–113), on June 15, 2016, the Director of National Intelligence, the Secretary of Homeland Security, the Secretary of Defense, and the Attorney General issued updated, final guidance on the sharing of cyber threat indicators and defensive measures among multiple Federal and non-Federal entities.

What was your impression of the guidance? Are there aspects that you find insufficient or impractical?

Answer. The chamber was impressed at the wide-spread support CISA/AIS stakeholders showed for the final CISA procedures and guidance documents that were released on June 15. The chamber especially commends DOJ's Leonard Bailey, senior counsel, and DHS's Gabe Taran, acting assistant general counsel for infrastructure programs, for their positive roles in negotiating with multiple parties and writing the documents under a tight deadline.

The chamber believes that the procedures and guidance are sufficient and practical.

Question 1b. In addition to resolving the question of liability protections for private-to-private sharing, are there other aspects of the DHS guidance that you believe would benefit from additional clarity?

Answer. The issue related to clarifying liability protections for private-to-private sharing seems to have been dealt with adequately. The procedures and guidance do not need additional clarification at this time. In the main, the chamber is urging industry to take advantage of CISA/AIS as appropriate.

Question 1c. Are there aspects of the law that should be clarified?

Answer. No. The CISA/AIS program is off to a good start. While oversight by Congress is crucial, it is too soon to make changes to the legislation. CISA does not need to be reauthorized until September 2025.

---

[2] *www.us-cert.gov/sites/default/files/ais_files/AIS_Terms_of_Use.pdf.*

[3] *http://media.wix.com/ugd/416668_2c6d85d4964743f8b4d3470b860f6e3b.pdf.*

[4] *https://hitrustalliance.net/hitrust-advances-State-cyber-threat-information-sharing-nations-healthcare-sector.*

The chamber urges lawmakers and the next administration to be industry's ally as it uses CISA/AIS, which is currently more important to businesses than clarifications. Companies need to trust that policy makers have their backs. It is important that businesses see that the protections granted by CISA—including matters tied to limited liability, regulation, antitrust, and public disclosure—become real. For some businesses, the protections are still an open question.

The chamber agrees with a witness who spoke on June 21 before the Commission on Enhancing National Cybersecurity at the University of California-Berkeley. He noted that the Government could make it easier for companies to create a "regulatory safe space," where they can more effectively share information about threats and attacks.[5]

The chamber hears such sentiments frequently and believes that Government entities like DHS want to use company data prudently. However, many more agencies and departments will have to adopt attitudes and actions that do not discourage businesses from reporting threat and vulnerability data.

Question 2. As a general rule, small- and medium-size businesses do not have the resources to devote to the most advanced, state-of-the-art information technology systems. As such, smaller enterprises may use older systems that have known cybersecurity vulnerabilities. Can these companies rely on older systems to share or receive threat information or do their platforms require a more advanced system?

Answer. The chamber's experience suggests that sophisticated cybersecurity programs can be very expensive to develop, deploy, and maintain for companies of all sizes, particularly small and mid-size businesses (SMBs).

DHS does not charge a fee for companies to participate in AIS. However, any AIS participant will need to adhere to defined technical connectivity activities, which DHS helps organizations manage.[6] Larger firms may have more resources to submit indicators directly through AIS. Most SMBs may not need to.

Indeed, the chamber anticipates that many SMBs will benefit from an innovative, automated-sharing ecosystem. A key long-term goal of information-sharing policy is to foster economies of scale in real-time, machine-to-machine sharing. The chamber anticipates that the marketplace will eventually provide inexpensive and easy-to-deploy technologies that conform to CISA's rules (e.g., scrubbing privacy information from CTIs) and generate and swap threat signatures at internet speeds. Systems like AIS will be able to block attacks sooner and more regularly, compared with the relatively human-intensive sharing schemes in use today.

The chamber understands that cyber threat intelligence companies have the means to enable companies to opt-in to AIS and gain from the process of receiving pertinent security event information such as IP addresses, domain names, hashes, and actor tactics, techniques, and procedures.

From a resource standpoint, it is probably too much to ask most SMBs to engage in the cybersecurity threat-sharing ecosystem directly. Many SMBs will likely struggle to create and maintain sound cybersecurity programs.[7] Technology may be challenging to use, and professional cyber talent is both scarce and pricey. Public policy does not do a sufficient job of recognizing the potentially extraordinary costs that industry faces in creating robust information-security programs.

Secretary of Commerce Penny Pritzker spoke at the chamber on September 27 concerning cybersecurity policy. She said that cyber space is the "only domain where we ask private companies to defend themselves" against foreign powers and other significant threats. She wondered aloud, "Does that sound as crazy to you as it does to me?"[8] Government does not stand between private entities and malicious hackers, she suggested.

It is instructive, according to a Council of Insurance Agents and Brokers market survey, that 26.1 percent of SMBs purchase "cyber" insurance for risk mitigation assistance (4.5 percent) and post-breach resources (21.6 percent). In contrast, 20.4 percent of large entities purchase "cyber" insurance for risk mitigation assistance (10.2 percent) and post-breach resources (10.2 percent).[9] In the chamber's view, companies typically have healthy and maturing cyber risk management programs in place before engaging in active information-sharing initiatives.

---

[5] *https://cltc.berkeley.edu/2016/06/27/cltc-hosted-white-house-commission-considers-challenges-opportunities-for-the-next-president.*

[6] *www.us-cert.gov/sites/default/files/ais_files/AIS_fact_sheet.pdf, www.us-cert.gov/sites/default/files/ais_files/AIS_FAQ.pdf.*

[7] *https://inthenation.nationwide.com/news/small-business-cyber-security-survey.*

[8] *www.commerce.gov/news/secretary-speeches/2016/09/us-secretary-commerce-penny-pritzker-delivers-keynote-address-us.*

[9] *www.ciab.com/news.aspx?id=6176.*

Question 3. In developing the aforementioned guidance, § 103(a)(5) specified that the procedures established must facilitate periodic circulation of cybersecurity "best practices" designed with special attention to the accessibility and implementation challenges faced by small businesses. Do the policies and procedures described in the guidance actually facilitate the development and circulation of best practices that are mindful of small business needs?

Answer. In keeping with section 103(a)(5) of CISA, the Federal Government-sharing guidance calls for the periodic sharing of cybersecurity best practices "with attention to accessibility and implementation challenges faced by small business concerns." The guidance outlines several programs, activities, and Federal agencies and departments that support the recurrent sharing of sound cybersecurity techniques, which are expected to be rooted in the on-going analyses of cyber threat data.

Here are some examples of cybersecurity best practices featured in the Federal Government-sharing guidance and that the chamber includes in our National cyber education campaign:

- *NIST Computer Security Division.*—NIST special publications and interagency reports, covering a broad range of topics, provide management, operations, and technical security guidelines for Federal agency information systems. Beyond these documents, which are peer reviewed throughout industry, Government, and academia, NIST conducts workshops, awareness briefings, and outreach to help ensure greater understanding of standards and guidelines resources.[10]
- *DHS Critical Infrastructure Cyber Community (C³) Voluntary Program.*—The C³ (pronounced "c cubed") Voluntary Program helps enhance critical infrastructure cybersecurity and encourage the adoption of the framework. The C³ Voluntary Program aids sectors and private organizations that want to use the framework by connecting them with cyber risk management tools offered by DHS, other Federal entities, and the private sector.[11]
- *DHS National Cybersecurity and Communications Integration Center (NCCIC).*—The NCCIC disseminates publications that recommend practices and standards for technical and nontechnical users. Information is available for Government users, as well as owners, operators, and vendors of industrial control systems.[12] In addition, the NCCIC includes information specifically focused on securing small business and home networks.[13]

  Through the US–CERT, a component of NCCIC, DHS offers the Cyber Resilience Review (CRR), a no-cost, voluntary, nontechnical assessment to help an organization evaluate its resilience and cybersecurity practices. The CRR may be conducted as a self-assessment or as an on-site assessment facilitated by DHS cybersecurity professionals.
- *Small Business Administration (SBA) Cybersecurity Website.*—The SBA provides information about cybersecurity best practices through its website, which features top tips, among other resources, that SMBs can use.[14]

Question 4. There is a natural tension between sharing threat indicators quickly to facilitate rapid response, and sharing only the most valuable information once it has been processed and analyzed. I understand that DHS uses the former, emphasizing volume and timeliness. Do you prefer this "time is of the essence" approach? In other words, how useful and actionable is the information you [a business or private organization] receive from DHS?

Answer. The chamber supports the "time is of the essence" mind-set. During the legislative debate concerning CISA, we opposed amendments that would attempt to address the "second scrub" issue by requiring DHS to perform another scrub of cyber threat data for personal information before disseminating indicators to appropriate Federal entities. So the speed of sharing is key.

Granting authority to DHS to conduct a second scrub is not inherently bad if viewed only through the vague lens of "privacy." But privacy is just one of several considerations in CISA. For example, when one understands that CTIs rarely if ever contain personal information, the second scrub would bog down the sharing of CTIs from businesses to the Federal entities that need them in a timely manner.[15]

---

[10] *www.nist.gov/itl/computer-security-division.*
[11] *www.dhs.gov/ccubedvp.*
[12] *https://ics-cert.us-cert.gov.*
[13] *www.us-cert.gov/home-and-business.*
[14] *www.sba.gov/cybersecurity.*
[15] *www.uschamber.com/sites/default/files/cisa__ctis__separating__fact__from__fiction__ - aug__19__final.pdf.*

A DHS privacy official said at the Cybersecurity Conference for Lawyers in September that if a CTI field "fails or is not completed fully" by a submitter, the whole indicator is not held back, which is constructive from a timeliness standpoint.[16]

Question 5. The Cybersecurity Act of 2015 contains numerous provisions designed to safeguard privacy and civil liberties by requiring, for instance, the scrubbing of personal information. Are private-sector organizations using their own systems to fulfill these obligations or relying on DHS mechanisms?

Answer. Section 104(d)(2) of CISA requires businesses to remove any information from a CTI or DM that it knows at the time of sharing to be personal information of a specific individual or information that identifies a specific individual who is not directly related to a cybersecurity threat before sharing that data with a Federal entity.[17]

Private organizations use their own technical capabilities to scrub indicators of personal information. It is worth noting that a DHS privacy official said at the Cybersecurity Conference for Lawyers that there is no "hard and fast list of privacy information that must be removed" from CTIs. CISA/AIS stakeholders need to consult the non-Federal entity guidance for scrubbing protocols. Scrubbing is "ultimately up to the company that is sharing the indicators," she added. The chamber instructs businesses to remove personal information from cyber threat data and not to rely on DHS mechanisms, which, among other things, may impede timely sharing efforts.

QUESTIONS FROM RANKING MEMBER CEDRIC L. RICHMOND FOR ROBERT MAYER

Question 1a. In accordance with § 103 and § 105(a)(4) of the Cybersecurity Act of 2015 (Pub. L. No. 114–113), on June 15, 2016, the Director of National Intelligence, the Secretary of Homeland Security, the Secretary of Defense, and the Attorney General issued updated final guidance on the sharing of cyber threat indicators and defensive measures between and among Federal and non-Federal entities.

What was your impression of the guidance and are there aspects that you find insufficient or impractical?

Question 1b. In addition to resolving the question of liability protections for private-to-private sharing, are there other aspects of the DHS guidance that you believe would benefit from additional clarity?

Question 1c. Are there aspects of the law that should be clarified?

Answer. As indicated in our testimony, we applaud DHS for its efforts to meet CISA's aggressive deadlines and for producing both interim and final guidance that provides additional evidence of the liability protections afforded under the Act. We now continue to focus our attention on evaluating the requirements and benefits associated with implementing CISA, and we expect that more companies will enter into arrangements for sharing cyber threat indicators and defensive measures through the new DHS portal.

Our member companies believe that no additional statutory clarification is required at this time and that it would be premature to open up CISA for amendment so soon after final passage. The process to reach consensus on the language in CISA, including the liability and privacy protection provisions, was a lengthy one. The law establishes an information-sharing structure, provides for liability and privacy protections, and more granular details about how sharing is conducted are better placed in implementation guidance, policies, and procedures.

We also recognize that over time issues may arise that would benefit from more clarification in the Federal guidance. Should that occur, we are confident that DHS will continue to work with the private sector through the current highly-collaborative process with appropriate dialogue on any potential future modifications to the guidance.

Question 2. As a general rule, small- and medium-sized businesses do not have the resources to devote to the most advanced, state-of-the-art information technology systems. As such, they are more likely to use older systems even if they exhibit known cybersecurity vulnerabilities. In developing its information-sharing program, has DHS provided a means for entities that rely on these older systems to share and receive threat information, or does their platform require more advanced system?

Answer. It is clearly the case that small communications carriers do not possess the same level of technical and financial resources that can be devoted exclusively

---

[16] *www.us-cert.gov/sites/default/files/ais_files/AIS_Submission_Guidance_Appendix_-A.pdf.*

[17] *www.us-cert.gov/sites/default/files/ais_files/Non-Federal_Entity_Sharing_Guidance_-%28Sec%20105%28a%29%29.pdf.*

to cybersecurity operations and technologies as do the large service providers. Still, they rely on the same vendors for hardware and software as their larger peers given that small service providers do not have the scope and scale to incent vendors to manufacture products specifically for their needs. DHS through the National Coordinating Center (NCC) and US–CERT work with the vendor community to publicize software updates and vulnerabilities—and this information is used by large and small operators alike.

Implementing Automated Information Sharing (AIS) capabilities for small business in the short term is impeded by the fact that most small businesses lack the ability to devote limited technical and capital resources to fully participate in the program at this juncture. However, over time, smaller entities will be likely to pool their resources and work through the existing Information Sharing and Analysis Centers (ISAC) and the Information Sharing and Analysis Organizations (ISAOs) that are currently under development. DHS seems to be approaching the implementation of AIS in a correct fashion by enrolling entities that have the deep technical know-how and capacity to engage operationally and to provide input for enhancing current capabilities that ensure that timely and actionable information is made available to program participants. We can also report that the communications sector, through a pilot effort under the auspices of CTIA, is working with a diverse set of industry participants (including small providers) to test the capabilities of AIS and the associated protocols and make modifications necessary to support telecommunications-specific requirements to support automated information sharing.

Question 3. In developing the aforementioned guidance, § 103(a)(5) specified that the procedures established must facilitate periodic circulation of cybersecurity "best practices" designed with special attention to the accessibility and implementation challenges faced by small businesses. Do the policies and procedures described in the guidance actually facilitate the development and circulation of best practices that are mindful of small business needs?

Answer. It is commonly understood that the small- and medium-sized businesses face substantial burdens when contemplating whether to share cyber threat indicators and defensive measures. The human resources and financial costs of participation can be daunting. However, we also recognize how important the small- and medium-sized businesses are in making the information-sharing environment effective. As DHS and industry gain a better understanding of the AIS process and its associated costs and benefits, small and medium businesses will be better-positioned to leverage experiences and lessons learned that are likely to be communicated and provided through their ISACs and any ISAO in which they participate.

It is also worth noting that for smaller companies, the current guidance does allow for sharing via means outside of the portal including via an email or phone call. This is especially important for this class of providers who may not be using technologies such as STIX and TAXI at this point in time. There needs to be continued flexibility inherent in the overall information-sharing process to accommodate the needs and capabilities of small- and medium-sized providers.

DHS might also want to consider convening a workshop with representatives of small entities to discuss current capabilities of AIS, the requirements to implement for smaller companies, the costs associated with implementation, the constraints that small companies face, and possible technical, operational, and administrative processes that may be streamlined to make participation for small entities more feasible.

Question 4. There is a natural tension between sharing threat indicators quickly to facilitate rapid response, and sharing only the most valuable information once it has been processed and analyzed. I understand that DHS uses the former, emphasizing volume and timeliness. Do you prefer this "time is of the essence" approach? In other words, how useful and actionable is the information you receive from DHS?

Answer. This may not be an either-or proposition though it is an important question. We often talk about information needing to be both "timely" and "actionable" which means that information can become quickly perishable and while it may be quality information, it may no longer be actionable. So it must be recognized that what is most important is that the information is accurate and provides the necessary context to facilitate specific action. We cannot lose these qualities for the sake of expediency.

The balance between what is timely and what is useful will continue to evolve based on the nature of the threat, and the nature of the type of information being shared. One of the primary purposes of sharing is to involve more parties to evaluate cyber threat indicators and defensive measures. As part of the collaborative nature of the information-sharing regime, we must all be mindful of the need for parties to strike the right balance between "timely" and "effective" information-sharing practices.

63

Having said that, we do value the DHS view that "time is of the essence" and over time, we have seen substantial improvements in the timeliness and utility of information shared with us by the Government. Information received from the Government is one of many resources that many of our member companies use as part of their own cybersecurity efforts. Generally speaking, we have no significant issues with the way that DHS is implementing the information sharing provisions of the Act. If issues arise, we expect that DHS and the private sector will address them in a collaborative way.

Question 5. The Cybersecurity Act of 2015 contains numerous provisions designed to safeguard privacy and civil liberties by requiring, for instance, the scrubbing of personal information. Are private-sector organizations using their own systems to fulfill these obligations or relying on DHS mechanisms?

Answer. The structure contemplated by CISA contains multiple layers of privacy protections for information sharing with the Federal Government and confers responsibilities on both the private sector and the Federal Government. The first layer places responsibility on a private sector entity sharing information to ensure it reviews the information for known personal information of a specific person, and if such information is present, that it is connected to a cybersecurity threat. Conversely, if it is not, the information must be removed.

The next layer of responsibility in the private-to-Federal venue is on the Federal Government at the point of receipt, and prior to sharing with other Federal entities. Our members take the responsibility placed upon them very seriously and understand that it is not sufficient or legally prudent to merely rely on the Federal Government to conduct its privacy review upon receipt of the information.

Moreover, some of our member companies have established, mature information-sharing mechanisms that long pre-date CISA and that also include strong privacy protective systems and practices. Those members will likely continue to rely on established methods to meet the baseline requirements concerning privacy protections under CISA, and to also go beyond those baseline requirements. Indeed, some members consider one step further than what is required under CISA. Namely once it has been established that it is legal under CISA to share cyber threat information that contains personal information, they will consider whether they should share it or could the cyber threat indicator be shared in a meaningful way without personal information? Our member companies will also rely on their privacy protective policies and practices in the private-to-private information sharing context, which does not contemplate DHS involvement or review.

Finally, the Automated Information Sharing (AIS) system DHS established to effectuate its role as the primary automated intake portal under CISA by design substantially minimizes the likelihood that personal information could, as a technical matter, be conveyed if it is not directly related to a cybersecurity threat. The technology, by design, adds another layer of privacy protection for companies sharing through the portal with DHS.

I hope that you find this information to be fully responsive to your questions.

QUESTIONS FROM RANKING MEMBER CEDRIC L. RICHMOND FOR MARK G. CLANCY

Question 1a. In accordance with § 103 and § 105(a)(4) of the Cybersecurity Act of 2015 (Pub. L. No. 114–113), on June 15, 2016, the Director of National Intelligence, the Secretary of Homeland Security, the Secretary of Defense, and the Attorney General issued updated final guidance on the sharing of cyber threat indicators and defensive measures between and among Federal and non-Federal entities.

What was your impression of the guidance and are there aspects that you find insufficient or impractical?

Question 1b. In addition to resolving the question of liability protections for private-to-private sharing, are there other aspects of the DHS guidance that you believe would benefit from additional clarity?

Question 1c. Are there aspects of the law that should be clarified?

Answer. As you mentioned, the updated guidance issued on June 15, 2016 on sharing for non-Federal entities [1] makes the important clarification needed about how protections still apply when sharing occurs between private-sector entities in Annex 1 "Sharing of Cyber Threat Indicator and Defensive Measure Sharing between Non-Governmental Entities under CISA". The guidance was extremely helpful to provide clarification for concerns previously raised with the interim guidance.

---

[1] Guidance to Assist Non-Federal Entities to Share Cyber Threat Indicators and Defensive Measures with Federal Entities under the Cybersecurity Information Sharing Act of 2015, June 2016.

As we have mentioned, we believe the U.S. Department of Homeland Security (DHS) has been very helpful in providing updates and clarifications. As we consider these questions, there are two areas that would also be helpful for DHS to provide some assistance. There are other programs within DHS that have been very helpful over time, the Cybersecurity Information Sharing and Collaboration Program (CISCP) and the Protected Critical Infrastructure Information Program (PCII).

While CISCP, PCII, and the Cybersecurity Information Sharing Act (CISA) have different statutory authorities, and over time were created for different reasons, as we consider broader cybersecurity information sharing there are overlaps and some growing questions about how the private sector should share information and which programs should be used.

First, it would be helpful for DHS to address how the CISCP program fits within the scope of the Automation Indicator Sharing (AIS) system and with CISA. The CISCP data is available as a separate 'feed' on the AIS system, however access to this feed requires a Cooperative Research and Development Agreement (CRADA) to be in place. Since CISCP is part of AIS, that would mean that sharing under CISCP would have the same protections under CISA as AIS and it would be important for DHS to confirm that point. If that is not accurate, then it would be helpful for DHS to provide that clarification in order to ensure that is the case.

Second, as we consider other aspects of the law and cybersecurity information sharing with DHS, it would be helpful for DHS to provide clarification on how the PCII program currently does, and in the future will, work with CISA. While PCII was created many years ago for physical events, it has morphed over time to include physical and cybersecurity events and is a useful program. Many companies, whether large or small, will need to understand and ultimately choose what program to share information through and clarification now would be important.

Question 2. As a general rule, small- and medium-sized businesses do not have the resources to devote to the most advanced, state-of-the-art information technology systems. As such, they are more likely to use older systems even if they exhibit known cybersecurity vulnerabilities. In developing its information-sharing program, has DHS provided a means for entities that rely on these older systems to share and receive threat information, or does their platform require more advanced system?

Answer. We work closely with a number of small- and medium-sized businesses and are providing answers to your questions based on our experience working with them. As you may expect, for those companies who are small- and medium-sized businesses, they may have different perspectives than we do. However, we have a few thoughts and suggestions on this question.

DHS has provided two additional methods for firms unable to use the automation to share information with the Department whether firms are small-, medium-sized, or larger ones not able to use automation. That includes a web submission form and an email box to send submissions. Both methods are accessible for small or medium business whether they are using older information technology systems or simply choose not to use automation. DHS could consider ways to share with organizations how that manual information will be shared back. It may also be helpful for DHS to provide guidance or best practices on how to craft a good submission. In fact, this may be useful for those sharing via an automated or manual submission.

Question 3. In developing the aforementioned guidance, § 103(a)(5) specified that the procedures established must facilitate periodic circulation of cybersecurity "best practices" designed with special attention to the accessibility and implementation challenges faced by small businesses. Do the policies and procedures described in the guidance actually facilitate the development and circulation of best practices that are mindful of small business needs?

Answer. One area that may be more challenging for small- and medium-sized businesses could be in understanding how to understand and manage "defensive measures." The guidance discussed how these will be created and what they contain. Small- and medium-sized businesses will have different abilities to understand how to manage them when they are received and may need additional support to create internal structures to implement them. Whether large or small, it would be helpful to have a method for providing feedback or surveying recipients (of such defensive measures) as to the level of detail that a company finds useful or lacking. In other instances in the past, suggestions may come from an agency that over-simplifies what defensive measure should be taken including "patch your systems," "update anti-virus," or "use a firewall." Suggestions for defensive measures from the U.S. Government going forward will need to be tailored to the size and abilities of the companies.

It is important to note that many small business use service providers to perform some or all of their IT services. These service providers are a community to which the Department must engage to effectively assist small businesses benefit from the information shared via CISA.

Question 4. There is a natural tension between sharing threat indicators quickly to facilitate rapid response, and sharing only the most valuable information once it has been processed and analyzed. I understand that DHS uses the former, emphasizing volume and timeliness. Do you prefer this "time is of the essence" approach? In other words, how useful and actionable is the information you receive from DHS?

Answer. There is an inherent tension between sharing quickly and sharing the most valuable information that no single approach will solve. However, sharing quickly with the ability to revise information shared when refined or after feedback from other parties is received is the optimal approach. Discussions have been had with DHS about adding ways to share confidence ratings within the cyber threat intelligence (CTI) AIS system that could be utilized to make the determination of how best to act on the information. As a result, CTI could be shared but if needed be matched with a lower confidence information versus those that may receive a higher high confidence based on information that has additional vetting imbedded in it.

Question 5. The Cybersecurity Act of 2015 contains numerous provisions designed to safeguard privacy and civil liberties by requiring, for instance, the scrubbing of personal information. Are private-sector organizations using their own systems to fulfill these obligations or relying on DHS mechanisms?

Answer. In our experience, the private sector firms Soltra works with take privacy very seriously and are taking the necessary steps to ensure that scrubbing of information is occurring before information is shared under CISA. The final DHS-DOJ guidance also does a good job providing examples of the demarcation under CISA on what data points may be related to the actual threat and how best to manage that process.

We appreciate all that you do on these issues. If you or your staff would like to discuss any of these matters in more detail, please let us know.

QUESTIONS FROM CHAIRMAN JOHN L. RATCLIFFE FOR MORDECAI ROSEN

Question 1. In your opinion, do DHS's programs to secure Federal Information Systems—Einstein and the Continuous Diagnostics and Mitigation (CDM) program—together offer a comprehensive solution and a defense-in-depth strategy to secure Federal networks?

Answer. Federal Information Systems are much safer today as a result of early implementation of the Einstein and CDM programs. The Federal Government has successfully integrated logical access through the use of the PIV card for all privileged users and performed an audit and reductions of privileged accounts. In particular, OPM has utilized the CDM roadmap whereby you start with identifying assets and users, then move toward managing behavior.

Early implementation of the Einstein program has helped Federal agencies to detect malicious cyber attacks, and to communicate these threats across the Federal Government.

However, there remain opportunities for improving security through automated response and modernization of antiquated legacy systems.

We think the Cyber Sprint helped improve Government security overall as well. Some say we need a marathon and we agree, there is much work to do. But, we believe that a long series of tightly measured sprints invokes management focus and unmatched operational cadence.

The Einstein and CDM programs constitute an effective strategy to improve Federal agency cybersecurity, with opportunities for continuous improvement as technology evolves. However, a plan and strategy are inconsequential without deployment. Deployment urgency will remain a critical component to maximizing protection of Federal networks.

Question 2. In your opinion, are DHS's cybersecurity programs for both Federal and non-Federal entities flexible and dynamic enough for it to leverage emerging cutting-edge technologies and to keep pace with the rapidly-evolving cyber threat landscape?

Answer. CA Technologies believes that DHS has become much stronger at engaging with stakeholders and incorporating private-sector input into both Federal and non-Federal cybersecurity programs. These include the Einstein and CDM programs for Federal agencies and the Automated Indicator Sharing (AIS) program for private entities.

This stakeholder engagement is vital to maintaining flexibility and incorporating cutting-edge technologies.

We believe the major challenge in maintaining pace with the evolving cyber threat landscape lies in the procurement, acquisition, and deployment process. In particular, we see a need for more and better-trained contracting personnel who have a strong understanding of modern technologies and are empowered to accelerate deployment of technologies under DHS programs.

Further we, and our technology industry partners, continue to advocate for stronger Federal Government alignment with the NIST-developed Framework for Improving Critical Infrastructure Cybersecurity, which envisions dynamic, flexible approaches to improving cybersecurity, and calls for continuous improvement based on evolving threat dynamics.

Question 3. A long-term goal of Einstein includes the filtering of email, HTTP traffic, and DNS sinkholing. What would your estimation be of the other security risks to Federal networks outside filtering email, HTTP traffic, and DNS sinkholing?

Answer. CA Technologies believes that the compromise of digital identities will continue to remain a primary security risk. Compromised identities have been a common thread in virtually every large network breach in recent years, including Federal agency breaches.

CA believes that identity and access management technologies are central to protecting systems, networks, devices, and data. As Federal agencies increase their utilization of digital technologies, the authentication of persons and the authentication of devices and data will remain crucial to protecting Federal networks.

In addition, authentication of both individuals and data will become increasingly important to maintaining the integrity of cyber threat information-sharing programs, as they are opened up to multiple actors and organizations.

Further, as the application economy continues to evolve, more organizations and governments will be opening up their data sets to third parties. Therefore, it will be critical to both effectively manage and secure the application programming interfaces that allow for these transactions.

QUESTIONS FROM RANKING MEMBER CEDRIC L. RICHMOND FOR MORDECAI ROSEN

Question 1a. In accordance with Sec. 103 and Sec. 105(a)(4) of the Cybersecurity Act of 2015 (Pub. L. No. 114–113), on June 15, 2016, the Director of National Intelligence, the Secretary of Homeland Security, the Secretary of Defense, and the Attorney General issued updated final guidance on the sharing of cyber threat indicators and defensive measures between and among Federal and non-Federal entities.

What was your impression of the guidance and are there aspects that you find insufficient or impractical?

Question 1b. In addition to resolving the question of liability protections for private-to-private sharing, are there other aspects of the DHS guidance that you believe will benefit from additional clarity?

Question 1c. Are there aspects of the law that should be clarified?

Answer. CA Technologies would like to congratulate DHS, ODNI, DOD, and DOJ on the job they have done in issuing updated final guidance on the sharing of cyber threat indicators and defensive measures between and among Federal and non-Federal entities.

The guidance clearly explains the mechanisms for sharing cyber threat information with the Federal Government, the requirements for removing personally identifiable information, and the liability protections that will be afforded to organizations that comply with the requirements of the legislation.

At this point, CA believes that stakeholders would benefit from further DOJ and DHS clarification of liability protections for actions taken in good faith participation in the information-sharing program. The Automated Indicator Sharing (AIS) program envisions a wide volume and velocity of shared cyber threat indicator data streams, which will require significant analysis in order to make them actionable. It is possible that some organizations will act on certain data streams that may ultimately prove not to be related to cyber threats, and other organizations may miss relevant indicators in the data streams, all while participating in good faith. Greater clarification of liability protections under these scenarios would benefit participants.

CA believes this clarification can be provided through DHS and DOJ outreach with stakeholders and potentially through further guidance. We don't believe the law needs to be clarified at this point.

Question 2. As a general rule, small- and medium-sized businesses do not have the resources to devote to the most advanced, state-of-the-art information technology systems. As such, they are more likely to use older systems even if they exhibit known cybersecurity vulnerabilities. In developing its information-sharing program, has DHS provided a means for entities that rely on these older systems to share and receive threat information, or does their platform require a more advanced system?

Answer. Our sense is that DHS has developed its information-sharing program in a way that allows for maximum participation with respect to manual sharing of cyber threat indicators. In addition to allowing organizations to share indicators through the AIS program, it also allows organizations to share cyber threat indicators through a web form or email. In order to receive liability protection under the law, these organizations will need to remove any personally identifiable information (PII) from information they share that they know at the time of sharing is not related to a cyber threat. This will require the organization to use manual controls or to implement automated controls to ensure PII is removed. Automated technologies, such as Application Programming Interface management software are available in the marketplace for small- and medium-sized businesses.

In order for small businesses to receive cyber threat indicators from the Federal Government in close to real time, they will need to sign up to the AIS program. This will require them to acquire a Trusted Automated eXchange of Indicator Information (TAXII) client and to receive a Public Key Infrastructure (PKI) certificate from an approved provider. This may be difficult for some small businesses. We recommend that DHS continue to conduct outreach and awareness raising with small businesses to help them properly understand how cybersecurity risks impact their overall business risk environment. This will help small businesses better prioritize cybersecurity investments, including potential participation in information-sharing programs.

Question 3. In developing the aforementioned guidance, Sec. 103(a)(5) specified that the procedures established must facilitate periodic circulation of cybersecurity "best practices" designed with special attention to the accessibility and implementation challenges faced by small businesses. Do the policies and procedures described in the guidance actually facilitate the development and circulation of best practices that are mindful of small business needs?

Answer. The guidance titled, "Sharing of Cyber Threat Indicators and Defensive Measures by the Federal Government under the Cybersecurity Information Sharing Act of 2015" included a section on periodic sharing of cybersecurity best practices. This section includes a listing of many cross-governmental programs, which provide cybersecurity guidance. Included in this list of programs are those with a focus on small- and medium-sized businesses such as those provided by US–CERT, the National Cybersecurity and Communications Integration Center (NCCIC), and the Small Business Administration.

CA believes that facilitating the development and circulation of best practices should remain a priority for DHS implementation of the Cybersecurity Act of 2015 in order to make Government cybersecurity programs more accessible and actionable for the full range of stakeholders. We would recommend that DHS continue to flesh out this section with additional guidance in future updates.

Question 4. There is a natural tension between sharing threat indicators quickly to facilitate rapid response, and sharing only the most valuable information once it has been processed and analyzed. I understand that DHS uses the former, emphasizing volume and timeliness. Do you prefer this "time is of the essence" approach? In other words, how useful and actionable is the information you receive from DHS?

Answer. CA Technologies is not currently a participant in the AIS program, however we are in the process of actively exploring engagement. At this point, we recognize the importance of emphasizing volume and timeliness. In the longer term, we believe it will be important to enable automated analysis of data in order to make it more actionable for organizations that don't have the resources to process and analyze massive data sets. Authentication of both program participants and the data that is shared will be a critical factor in the successful implementation of this program.

Question 5. The Cybersecurity Act of 2015 contains numerous provisions designed to safeguard privacy and civil liberties by requiring, for instance, the scrubbing of personal information. Are private-sector organizations using their own systems to fulfill these obligations or relying on DHS mechanisms?

Answer. CA Technologies' understanding of the Cybersecurity Act of 2015, and its related guidance, is that it requires organizations to scrub personal information that they know, at the time of sharing, is not related to a cybersecurity threat in order to receive liability protection under the law. CA Technologies is not a current participant in the AIS program though we are currently actively exploring participation. Should we participate in the program, we would use our own systems to fulfill privacy obligations before sharing cyber threat indicators with the Government.

As we noted in our answer to question No. 2, there are existing technologies available in the marketplace to help organizations filter personally identifiable informa-

68

tion from data sets before sharing with the Government. We anticipate that most organizations will want to utilize these automated technologies or will implement manual controls to remove personal information before sharing. The DHS mechanisms will then provide an additional level of privacy assurance.

QUESTIONS FROM RANKING MEMBER CEDRIC L. RICHMOND FOR OLA SAGE

Question 1a. In accordance with § 103 and § 105(a)(4) of the Cybersecurity Act of 2015 (Pub. L. No. 114–113), on June 15, 2016, the Director of National Intelligence, the Secretary of Homeland Security, the Secretary of Defense and the Attorney General issued updated final guidance on the sharing of cyber threat indicators and defensive measures between and among Federal and non-Federal entities.
What was your impression of the guidance and are there aspects that you find insufficient or impractical?
Question 1b. In addition to resolving the question of liability protections for private-to-private sharing, are there other aspects of the DHS guidance that you believe would benefit from additional clarity?
Question 1c. Are there aspects of the law that should be clarified?
Answer. Response was not received at the time of publication.
Question 2. As a general rule, small- and medium-sized businesses do not have the resources to devote to the most advanced, state-of-the-art information technology systems. As such, they are more likely to use older systems even if they exhibit known cybersecurity vulnerabilities. In developing its information-sharing program, has DHS provided a means for entities that rely on these older systems to share and receive threat information, or does their platform require more advanced system?
Answer. Response was not received at the time of publication.
Question 3. In developing the aforementioned guidance, § 103(a)(5) specified that the procedures established must facilitate periodic circulation of cybersecurity "best practices" designed with special attention to the accessibility and implementation challenges faced by small businesses. Do the policies and procedures described in the guidance actually facilitate the development and circulation of best practices that are mindful of small business needs?
Answer. Response was not received at the time of publication.
Question 4. There is a natural tension between sharing threat indicators quickly to facilitate rapid response, and sharing only the most valuable information once it has been processed and analyzed. I understand that DHS uses the former, emphasizing volume and timeliness. Do you prefer this "time is of the essence" approach? In other words, how useful and actionable is the information you receive from DHS?
Answer. Response was not received at the time of publication.
Question 5. The Cybersecurity Act of 2015 contains numerous provisions designed to safeguard privacy and civil liberties by requiring, for instance, the scrubbing of personal information. Are private-7sector organizations using their own systems to fulfill these obligations or relying on DHS mechanisms?
Answer. Response was not received at the time of publication.

○

www.ingramcontent.com/pod-product-compliance
Lightning Source LLC
Chambersburg PA
CBHW081240280526
45787CB00006B/2736